Decorating Texas

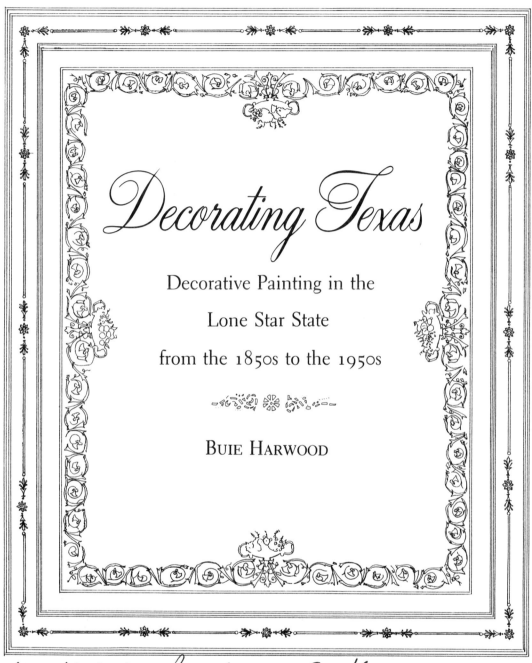

Decorating Texas

Decorative Painting in the

Lone Star State

from the 1850s to the 1950s

BUIE HARWOOD

For Virginia Buchanan-Smith —

Texas Christian University Press
FORT WORTH

Your brother Lester was a strong supporter of this project, so I am pleased that he is giving you a copy of my book! Enjoy!
Buie Harwood

Library of Congress Cataloging-in-Publication Data

Harwood, Buie.
  Decorating Texas : decorative painting in the Lone Star State from
the 1850s to the 1950s / by Buie Harwood.
    p.   cm.
  Includes bibliographical references.
  ISBN 0-87565-113-5. — ISBN 0-87565-114-3
    1. Mural painting and decoration, American — Texas.   2. Decoration
and ornament, Architectural — Texas.   3. Color in architecture —
Texas.   4. Façades — Texas.   I. Title.
ND2635.T4H37   1993
729'.4'0976409034—dc20   92-38053
                                                                  CIP

Designed by Barbara Whitehead

Unless otherwise indicated, all the illustrations in this
book are in the author's collection.

CONTENTS

To my Mom and Dad, for my education;
To my grandmothers, Babe and Mimi, for their historical legacy;
To my students, for their interest and encouragement;
To the artistic creators who provided an
enriching source of inspiration.

Acknowledgements

My SINCERE THANKS to various people for their encouragement, assistance, and interest. Special thanks to former colleagues Anna Brightman in interior design and Wayne Bell in architecture, University of Texas at Austin, for the initial contacts that provided inspiration for this project.

The measured drawing work was completed by interior design students participating in the University of Texas Winedale Institute in Historic Preservation. Many thanks to former students Catherine Suttle, Sarah Brooks Eilers, Sally Parsley Condara, Tina Howard Leva, Linda Flory, Sue Mitchell, Cindy Hutchinson Taylor, Becky Hart, Cynthia Blue, Anne Moore, Hing Yue, Sherlop Prellop, Ella Parks, Karen Herbst, Barbara Redmon, Cathy Butcher, Sarah Klusczinski, Becky Hale, Mary Maier, and Kathy Mensik.

Advice and encouragement has been provided by friends and professional associates Ardis Rewerts, Cindy Brandimarte, Peter Flagg Maxson, Martha Freeman, John and Candy Volz, Amy Donaldson, and by county historical chairmen around the state. Thanks also to archivists Sandra Tatman of the Philadelphia Atheneum; Pat Eldredge, Sherwin Williams Company; Sister Delores Kasner, Catholic Archives in Austin; Ofelia Tennant, Catholic Archives in San Antonio; Virginia Mecklenburg, National Museum of American Art, Smithsonian Institution; and Arlene Platt of the General Services Administration.

This book would not have made it to press without the support and encouragement of Judy Alter and Tracy Row at Texas Christian University Press. At a time of great frustration, they saw value in the project and provided the assistance to make it happen. Their advice has been most beneficial. A special thanks to Tracy for his editing help and understanding.

The scope and depth of this book would not have been possible without the generous assistance provided by the building owners. I am most appreciative of their time and help. Thanks to all for their growing awareness of decorative painting, as it has reinforced my sense of purpose. This book is for those who enjoy ornamentation as a thing of beauty.

Funding and support for the research for *Decorating Texas* has been generously provided by: the National Endowment for the Arts, Washington, D.C. (Design Arts Program); University of North Texas, Denton (Organized Research Funds); Reed and Pate Foundation, Dallas (Grant through the Interior Design Educators Foundation); Texas Society of Architects, Austin (Architectural History Grant).

Buie Harwood
Richmond, Virginia
June 1992

Preface

FROM 1974 to 1985, I crisscrossed Texas researching decorative painting. The result is an inventory of over 350 structures that have original or altered ornamentation. Many illustrations remain simply because they were appreciated as creations of beauty. Ironically, others remain simply because they were covered over. Others have been restored. Unfortunately, many examples were destroyed during attempts at modernization, and as rehabilitation processes continue, further artifacts will be in imminent danger of complete destruction.

No previous effort had been made to locate, identify, record, document, and interpret decorative painting in Texas as it is represented in this survey. Decorated historic interiors are sometimes difficult to study: structures change over the years; documentation is often scanty; and certain types of buildings do not give the outward appearance of being decorated, although they are. Often, I found examples of decoration through "word of mouth" or written communication, since public records do not generally describe interiors.

My objective was to document site locations, decoration, colors, painting techniques, and the artists over one hundred years, and to produce a reference catalog. I chose to end the investigation at 1950 because the concept of decorative painting changed, support for federal arts projects diminished, and international art movements began to reflect new design directions.

Decorating Texas provides a broad survey with an emphasis on a wide variety of individual buildings, which exhibit an assortment of interiors and decorations by many different artists. Examples of decorative painting represent the typical and unique, high style and vernacular, elaborate and simple. Case studies illustrate work by various artists in a particular locale and for a particular building. Documentation and identification of artists prior to 1900 is extremely difficult, because so much of the work is anonymous. Often, information is limited because of the inaccuracies of the oral history or the unavailability of written records. Rare indeed was the prominence of an artist, the significance of a site, or the date of a decoration important enough for names and other data to have been recorded.

In developing this volume, I used guidelines and procedures gleaned from art historians, architects, interior designers, photographers, and government agencies. All measured drawings are the work of my students at the Winedale Institute in Historic Preservation, the University of Texas at Austin and follow instructions published by the Historic American Buildings Survey, Department of the Interior in Washington, D.C.

For readers who wish to examine and document interior ornamentation in their area, I offer the following suggestions.

Preliminary Investigation: Locate sites through written, oral, and visual contact; identify appropriate persons associated with the structures; list meaningful resources in the area.

Site Survey: Investigate the site for content of decorative painting; record historical information about the building; photograph paintings; measure decorative painting with particular attention to patterns and motifs; document paint colors using the Munsell Color Code system; identify and record the types of decoration and areas of use; interview persons associated with the structure to record oral histories of the sites.

Research: Take oral histories from family members of the painters; investigate family records and materials; investigate county courthouse, city, and state records; review city directories for references to particular owners or painters; check cemetery and census records associated with owners and artists; survey newspapers, journals, magazines, and trade catalogs; examine archives, library, and museum collections for private papers, family records, monographs, and architectural collections; investigate general and specific reference books concerning decorative painting, a particular structure, an artist, an owner, or a style.

Specific Inventory Content: Include the common and proper name of the structure; locate the building by county, city, and street; identify the original owner, present owner, and any important interim owners with background information; date the building and the decoration; identify the architect; identify the artist.

Analysis of Data: Identify and compare all information gathered; examine the impact of aesthetics and design; evaluate the rarity or placement within a local or regional context; evaluate the historical significance based on the owner, architect, structure, and artist; evaluate the concept of style and taste within the cultural and social framework.

"The term decoration signifies the art
or process of applying the
various elements to
beautify objects."

A *Handbook of Ornament*
Fran Sales Meyer,
1888

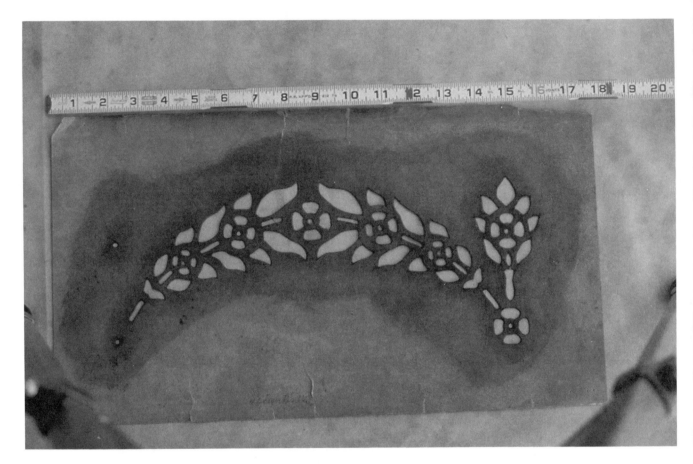

Stencil by Everett Edward Finigan, San Antonio. Transplanted Irishman Everett Edward Finigan (February 19, 1889–1969) was a master painter who worked primarily in San Antonio, Corpus Christi, and East and West Texas from the 1920s to the 1940s. Following in his father's footsteps, his designs for stencils were cut to fit a particular job. Sizes vary from 1'–4" wide to 2'–4" wide by 4" high to 10" high. Made of heavy brown waxed paper covered with varnish, the stencils show registration marks for centering the pattern. *(Courtesy Mrs. Howard Reischling, San Antonio.)*

ONE

A Texas Perspective

Decorative painting from the 1850s to the 1950s provides an artistic heritage for Texas, reflecting cultural influences, regional interpretations, and varied stylistic expressions through different historical periods. Decorative painting beautifies residential, religious, and commercial structures. These buildings vary in style, design, character, location, and date, and decorations mirror architectural diversity. Whatever the type of art — stencilling, infill painting, freehand painting, graining, or marbling — it shapes the overall interior design. The character may be vernacular, regional, or high style, and it often reflects the abilities of the artist, whether itinerant, in-state, or imported. In studying this diversity, one peers into the varied personalities of Texas.

Reflecting central European ideas, traditional concepts, and popular interests, decorative painting portrays an artistic album of Texas design and interprets many historic developments. This album includes styles of the frontier, Greek Revival, Victorian, the Arts and Crafts Movement, Art Nouveau, Colonial and Classical Revival, Spanish Colonial Revival, and Art Deco (which appears most often in post offices and movie theaters).

Within the five-state region of Texas, New Mexico, Louisiana, Arkansas, and Oklahoma, Texas has the most extant examples of decorative painting. Distributed all over the state, some examples can be found in buildings standing along major transportation and communication routes. But many are located in central Texas around the earliest and most continuous settlements, with fewer existing in the south and west. Early examples survive in rural areas because of strong ancestral ties and in middle-class locales because of less commercial intrusion and new construction. Later examples survive primarily because of appreciation or historic preservation.

The location of the building frequently affects the particular decorative interpretation. In rural areas, decoration may be simple, personal, vernacular, and ethnic.

1

Owners often commissioned local or itinerant artists to depict ancestral or popular images. If located in a middle-class environment, the decoration usually imitated regional or national influences with local or regional artists often following published resource materials and guidelines. If found in an urban area, decoration reflected wealth, education, and high style. The owners often hired prominent in-state artists or imported them from out of state.

The Buildings

Residential, religious, and commercial buildings in Texas provide a repository for decorative painting and influence the overall contextual image. The particular style of the structure may dictate the interior character, and the character may delineate the visual representation. Usually, there is an integral relationship between the building form and the decorative ornamentation, indicating a conceptual marriage between the two. When the image is expected, the decoration is "typical"; when the image is not expected, it is "unique." It is more typical to see a decorative Victorian church with elaborate ceiling treatments, for instance, than a commercial building decorated with fish murals.

Dating from the 1880s to the 1920s, remaining examples of decorative painting in Texas residential structures range from vernacular to high style, with images varying substantially in style, design, character, location, and date. Although found all over the state, many images are in Austin, Fayette, Washington, and Bexar counties. Several towns retain numerous examples of work by a single artist, as illustrated in Lindenau, Cistern, Brenham, and Dallas. Usually, the purpose of the painting was to decorate a surface, display wealth, or copy trends. Depending on the social status of the owners, buildings range from three-room dwellings to ten-room mansions. Some are formal and elaborate while others are informal and plain. Most, however, illustrate an integrated relationship between the proportion of the interior and the scale of the decoration through placement, motifs, colors, and details.

Residential structures illustrating typical images include the McGregor-Grimm House at Winedale, the Knoelle-Schroeder House in Industry, the Addison-Gandy House in Montgomery, and the Burton-Merritt House in McKinney. Those providing a unique interpretation include the Gluck-Kadernoschka Place in Cat Spring, the Eichholt-Guderian-Kruse House in the Brenham area, and the Kruppa-Zimmerhanzel House in Cistern.

Extant illustrations of decorative painting in religious structures created between the 1880s and the 1920s range from vernacular to high style, with national, European, ethnic, and regional images. A number of extraordinary examples survive in small towns and rural areas near Schulenburg. Since these buildings were usually the most prominent structures in the community, they often served as meeting places, as well as houses of worship. Most are classical or Gothic in design and decorated to match. Often an artist of European lineage painted the interior for a Catholic congregation of his own ethnic origin. Decoration usually appears on interior walls or ceiling surfaces and on apse spandrels and walls where it can be viewed by the congregation. The subjects are religious, decorative, or a combination of both. Religious symbols, along with depictions of saints and angels, provide inspiration for parishioners.

Typical images can be seen in Annunciation Catholic Church in Houston and Ascension Church in Moravia. Those providing unique interpretations include Wesley Brethren Church in Wesley, St. Mary's Catholic Church in High Hill, and St. Mary's Catholic Church in Umbarger.

Surviving illustrations of decorative painting in commercial structures date from the 1920s to the 1940s and usually portray regional, national, and high style designs. Although many examples remain in prominent downtown metropolitan buildings of Dallas, Austin, and Houston, the majority are in modest structures like post offices, office buildings, theaters, libraries, hotels, and schools. As public spaces, the interiors change frequently in response to use, style, or ownership. Generally, a lobby or a major public area contains decoration, often on an upper wall or ceiling surface. Blending with the architectural form, it usually includes murals and geometric motifs on a large scale and was executed by an in-state artist.

Some typical images include those in the Chemistry Building at the University of Texas at Austin, the Village Theater in Dallas, the city hall in Houston, and the post office in San Antonio. Those providing a unique interpretation include the Champion Store and Restaurant in Port Isabel and Parker Brothers Motor Company in Center.

The Interiors

Interior walls, ceilings, and floors provide the contextual envelope for the decorative painting. Appropriate placement of decoration on these architectural elements often contributes to the successful design. The artist controls the design through attention to space type, scale, surface material, paint medium, composition, pattern, color, and light.

A close correlation often exists between building design, decorative painting, and prevailing fashion. It is common to see structural areas divided into geometric sections. Walls, for instance, may be divided vertically into three sections based on classic proportions to depict a frieze band, a columned area, and a dado. Usually, the frieze is the most decorated section and delineates period characteristics. Ceilings are often divided into a perimeter zone and a center space with a medallion, the zone or border often copying the imagery of the frieze design. Floors are the least decorated element because of wear caused by circulation patterns. As with walls and ceilings, floors are often divided into geometric shapes.

These architectural elements become more prominent in certain spaces because of their scale and location. In residential structures, the parlor — usually a small space near the entry — may have extensive ornamentation because the owner wanted to impress visitors. This is exemplified by the Sterrett House in Beckville. In religious structures the nave and apse areas — large spaces in direct view — were decorated with spiritual symbols and paintings of biblical events. This is appropriately depicted in Ascension Church in Moravia and St. Mary's Catholic Church in Umbarger. In commercial buildings, the entry and lobby spaces — typically grand spaces with much traffic — contain the most embellishment so as to command attention. Examples can be found in the Village Theater in Dallas and in the San Antonio post office.

Within all these interiors, decorated surface materials vary substantially. Fixed or moveable (as in the case of canvas), they help create and enhance the decorative character. Preferred or popular surfaces in Texas include wood, plaster, and canvas. Common in older buildings are walls, ceilings and floors covered with wooden planks. Plaster surfaces — typical in all periods — are usually smooth or textured finishes on walls and ceilings. After 1900, canvas offered the artist an opportunity to work in a studio or on location, with eventual placement on walls or ceilings. Texas artists preferred to cover these surfaces with water-based paints (also known as distemper) or oil-based substances obtained in a powdered or liquid state.

Generally defined by the architectural form, decorative compositions usually follow standard formats within any given historical period. As design features, they illustrate stencilling, infill painting, and freehand painting, which appear as patterns or large surface treatments. Published guidelines addressed patterns placed over prominent architectural features, pattern scale relative to room size, and color manipulation based on character. Pattern sizes vary from 9″ wide by 3″ high to 2′ – 0″ wide by 1′ – 6″ high. Work by a single artist in several structures frequently shows repetition of the same patterns and sometimes the same colors. As an alternative, panel compositions covering large surface areas may offer isolated vignettes or individual paintings.

Color and light are interrelated design tools for a decorative artist. Color is defined by hue (color name), value (light or dark), and intensity (bright or dull). Light may be natural (from the sun) or artificial (kerosene, gas, or electric), with a bright or dim quality. Dark colors make rooms appear small and contained, while light colors have the opposite effect, a concept illustrated by period interiors. Intense colors, for instance, with distinctive contrasts appear more frequently during the Victorian period when interiors were dim because of kerosene or gas lighting. Pastels with fewer contrasts appear more at the turn of the century when interiors became brighter with electric lighting. Color also imitates specific materials such as graining or marbling.

Decoration

The type of decoration shapes the overall interior design and character of decorative painting. Reflecting influences from national models, examples studied in Texas include stencilling, infill painting, freehand painting, graining, and marbling. Extant examples define a style through various motifs, pictorial images, linear compositions, architectural placements, and colors. From the 1860s to the 1920s, stencilling and infill were more common in residential and religious structures, particularly around the turn of the century. Between the turn of the century and the 1940s, examples of freehand painting are more common in religious and commercial structures, seen particularly in the former during the 1900s and in the latter during the 1930s and 1940s. Graining and marbling are very limited, but show diverse interpretations on architectural features and date primarily to the late nineteenth century.

The design and character of stencilling and infill painting are very similar, generally differing only in scale and use. Stencilling is a mechanical process characterized by repeated patterns conveyed in a flat, unshaded manner. Divided into various parts, patterns require different stencil plates for each separate color, with the portion cut away defining the pattern. This concept is similar to the relationship of a negative and a photograph. Individual patterns may expand to create repetition, as illustrated in frieze borders. Common forms of stencilling are the block or solid stencil and the outline stencil, also referred to as infill painting or pounce painting.

The block or solid stencil typically had an entire pattern cut out, producing a complete design, as found in the stencils of Texas artist Everett Edward Finigan. The outline stencil, on the other hand, had an enlarged scale and telltale guidelines. Patterns were transferred by moving a pencil, a piece of charcoal, or a brush along the inner edge of a large open stencil, thereby creating a pattern outline on the surface. Upon removing the stencil, the artist filled in the design by hand. This technique is illustrated by the work of Fred Donecker and Sons and in the First Presbyterian Church in Galveston. Somewhat different in effect, pounce painting required small holes placed along the pattern perimeter with charcoal rubbed through them to transfer the design to a surface.

Many kinds of stencils appear in Texas, particularly those identified as detached, band, divider, and binder; all are exemplified by the work of artist Charles Martin Meister in Brenham. His compositions usually included corner and center motifs (detached), repetitive linear patterns (band), monochromatic border motifs (divider), and painted moldings (binder). Particularly scarce in Texas, all-over stencil patterns incorporated diaper-repeat-like wallpaper designs, with the motif repeated across the entire surface. Often the pattern was a darker or lighter shade of the background color, as depicted in several residential structures in Lindeau. Background stencils with a reverse positive and negative configuration are also scarce, but fine examples can be found in the Elks Lodge in Fort Worth and in the Landa House in San Antonio.

Freehand painting expressed the artist's individuality, with pictorial images conveyed through murals, scenics, or small compositions. Usually these images reflect the building's design, character, and function. Such decoration in Texas varies significantly. Memorable paintings include landscape scenes in the Gluck-Kadernoschka Place in Cat Spring, religious subjects presented in Annunciation Catholic Church in Houston and in St. Mary's Catholic Church in Umbarger, historical allegory in the State of Texas Building in Dallas and in the post office in San Antonio, and European imagery in the Burton-Merritt House in McKinney.

Graining and marbling create trompe l'oeil effects through the imitation of real wood or marble. Precise imitation of a costly material was difficult, requiring the expertise of a master craftsman. Following the fashion of the day, examples of graining appeared on doors, baseboards, and moldings, while those of marbling appeared on columns and mantels. Since these architectural features were often repainted, examples in Texas are limited. Using guidelines prescribed in national publications, graining with combs or rollers copied local or regional woods like walnut and oak. Various shades of brown with gold or rust undertones imitated typical straight-grain and burl cuts, as in the Addison-Gandy House in Montgomery. Marbling was an attempt by the artist to duplicate specific types of stone from white vein to Italian pink to varied local interpretations. Typical designs often have monochromatic colors, irregular spacing, and line variety. Such decorations are prominent in St. Paul's Lutheran Church in Serbin and St. Mary's Catholic Church in High Hill.

The Artists

The artists, often classified as decorative painters, represented various ethnic groups, including Swiss, German, Irish, French, Norwegian, Italian, Swedish, Czech, Mexican, and Anglo-American. Settling in rural as well as urban areas, they located where work was available or they had friendship ties. While settlement patterns for the artists can be dated and recorded by nationality, little substantive data exist to clarify individual names, identities, or where they chose to locate.

One way to distinguish between decorative painters is through their travels and work. They can be classified as "itinerant," "in-state," or "imported."

As the term suggests, itinerant artists moved from place to place around the country, seeking work wherever they could find it. Very little is known about them — in most cases not even their names — but by studying where they worked and their painting styles, it is possible to identify their ethnic backgrounds. Oral tradition typically documents a few personal characteristics. In the Gluck-Kadernoschka Place in Cat Spring and the Sterrett House in Beckville, for example, the simple style, ethnic flavor and personal expression indicates that the artist was from central Europe, yet knew some Texas and United States history. One story about the Rogers-Drummond House in Mount Vernon provides little commentary on a male artist. Commissioned to decorate the sixteen-foot-square parlor, he lived with the family for a year, but provided only limited and simple graining and stencilling for a classical Greek Revival house. In essence, he worked a long time, accomplished little, and did not relate the decoration to the style and character of the structure — a high style house built for a prominent family.

While in-state artists worked and lived primarily in Texas, many came from other areas of the country and from Europe. Some developed significant reputations — their compositions reflecting greater individuality, originality, and design planning than many other artists. As a result, some acquired more work in other states. Charles Martin Meister in Brenham, the Donecker family of San Antonio, Eugene John Gilboe in Austin and Dallas, and many of the post office muralists fall into this category. Early city directories list these artists under the category of "Painters/House, Sign, and Ornamental," while those of the 1920s list them as "Painters and Decorators," and directories of the 1940s list them as "Muralists and Scene Artists." The change in terminology represents a growing separation of roles based on expertise and the development of professional organizations like the Master House Painters and Decorators Association and the National Society of Mural Painters.

Imported artists from the metropolitan areas of the United States and Europe traveled widely, knew current styles and were commissioned based on their expertise and artistic reputation. They often worked in areas briefly, as in the case of Italian artist Peter Plotkin. Hired to decorate five rooms in the Burton-Merritt House in McKinney, he stayed just nine months but left a high style panorama of European-inspired figures and landscapes. The work of Oidtman Studios, a New York City firm, provides a similar example. Commissioned to decorate several central Texas churches during the 1930s, their artists stayed in each town for a few months, copied current published designs, provided a noteworthy catalog of religious landscapes, then moved on.

Prominent artists often identified themselves by signature. But the majority of decorative painters working in Texas before 1900 did not sign their work, or they worked anonymously for recognized firms. The identity of these artists frequently depends on their legacy through family records and local prominence. One exception to this, illustrated in the Dahse-Halla House in Weimar, is the signature of "W. Kolbe Maler" in a center medallion on the parlor ceiling. It became more common after 1900 for artists to sign their work, which is exemplified by many of the post office murals. The identity of these painters also frequently appears in city directories, government and institution records, private archives, photographic documentation, oral histories, and estate inventories. The number of artists listed increased significantly in growing areas where there was more competition for work.

Lewis House, Winedale. Stencilling, infill painting, freehand painting are by Rudolph Melchior, ca. 1850s–1860s. *(Drawing, courtesy University of Texas at Austin, Architectural Drawings Collection, Winedale Institute in Historic Preservation.)*

TWO

Influences: 1850 – 1900

BETWEEN 1850 and 1900, Texas grew into a more unified whole with improved transportation systems linking and expanding both rural and urban environments. This expansion increased significantly after the Texas Revolution, continued with statehood, and developed dramatically by the century's end. Popular architectural forms reflected frontier expressions, as well as the Greek Revival and Victorian styles. Although varying from high style to vernacular, most surviving buildings show a distinct emphasis on vernacular and ethnic interpretations as diverse cultural influences continued to shape decorative painting. Decoration dominates residential structures during this period, although a few commercial buildings also include ornamentation.

Most structures were located in central Texas along the improved waterways and popular roads, and today many are found in distinct ethnic communities and reflect their ethnic origins. Anglo settlers from the East Coast frequently populated Louisiana border towns like Jefferson and San Augustine, establishing themselves as landowners and merchants. European immigrants included Germans, Czechs, and Frenchmen. Leaving their homeland for economic reasons, they clustered in isolated rural communities. Numerous Germans established themselves as farmers and artisans throughout Galveston, Brenham, Fredericksburg, New Braunfels, and San Antonio. Following a similar pattern, Czechs arrived from Bohemia and Moravia and took up farming or small business operations in Cat Spring, Fayetteville, La Grange, Praha, and Wesley. Many French families settled south of San Antonio in the farm villages of Castroville and Lacoste, while others prospered commercially in Nacogdoches, Austin, Denton, and Dallas. Mexican colonists filtered throughout south Texas, concentrating in the Catholic mission towns of San Antonio, Goliad, and Laredo.

Settlement patterns also clarify architectural traditions. Despite time lags in influences, ethnic features dominated early Texas architecture. Log and wood-framed

9

frontier structures multiplied as the population expanded, but few examples survive. Remaining examples date from the 1830s to the 1860s, with decorative painting in them completed between the 1850s and the 1880s. Most were homes in the farm communities of Austin and Fayette counties — the area of the earliest Anglo and European settlements. Distinctive in their vernacular interpretations, houses are small, simple and often owned by German or Czech settlers. The decorative arts are usually variations of stencilling and infill painting through frieze borders, but there are notable exceptions.

Two examples — which include more ornamentation than most early frontier homes — are the Lewis House (ca. 1850s) at Winedale and the Knolle-Schroeder House (ca. 1868) in Industry. The former displays elaborate work by local resident Rudolph Melchior, while the latter illustrates simple decoration by an unknown itinerant artist. Following prescribed layouts, both incorporate stencilling, infill painting, and some freehand painting on wood wall, frieze, and ceiling surfaces. Marbling also decorates the dados in several public spaces. Colors vary, often imitating popular Victorian or ethnic influences. Contrasting with this painted imagery, the Gluck-Kadernoschka Place (ca. 1860s) in Cat Spring had two rooms with elaborate wall murals executed by an unknown itinerant artist. As a typical frontier architectural representation, this decoration was distinguished by subdued freehand images of European landscape scenes and of the old Texas state capitol.

Reflecting significant advances in the middle-class lifestyle, Texas buildings often imitated traditional Greek Revival forms but added some vernacular interpretations. The style was fully developed on the East Coast by 1850 and continued to grow as the southern plantation culture matured and people moved westward. Builders based their works on intellectual images and forms derived from classical antiquity, which had been refined by men such as Thomas Jefferson, William Stickland, Charles Bulfinch, Benjamin Henry Latrobe, and others. Symmetry and formality articulated beauty through temple fronts, white facades, and monumental scale. Interiors mirrored the moldings, and mantels. Often public areas are more elaborately decorated than private rooms. Accommodating various interpretations, the high style buildings were frequently designed by noted architects, while those in rural locales were often designed and constructed by local builders. A German emphasis predominates, but a lack of documentation hinders comparisons.

As the popular image of the intellectual Greek Revival shifted to the decorative Victorian, Texas buildings with decorative painting began to copy national models. These models emphasized historic styles and incorporated symbols of the past, including Gothic, Rococo, and Italian Renaissance. Picturesque eclecticism, stylistic mixture, excessive decoration, additive ornament, and mass production characterized most structures. Important designers included Andrew Jackson Downing, Alexander Jackson Davis, John Henry Belter, and Charles Eastlake as well as decorative painter John LaFarge.

The growing middle class read and was influenced by publications like *The American Woman's Home* (1869), *Hints on Household Tastes* (1877), *Godey's Lady's Book* (1830 – 1898), *The House Beautiful* (1881), *The Ladies' Home Journal* (1883), and *The Decoration of Houses* (1897). Victorian brick, wood, and stone buildings were architecture of exteriors, with classical wall divisions and details dominating the visual impression. Pale but intense colors of blue, green, salmon, yellow, and white softly radiated from wall and ceiling surfaces.

Numbering less than fifteen, the only Texas Greek Revival structures that still survive are residences dating from the 1840s to the 1870s; interior ornamentation dates from the 1840s to the 1900s. Most are in southeast Texas and were originally located on bustling transportation routes in thriving Anglo or German communities. Some exhibit high style design, but some are simple, perhaps reflecting the builder's knowledge and the owner's financial position. Decorated several years after construction, approximately half reflect Victorian influences in the interior. The decoration either exhibits graining or blends classical designs with Victorian motifs. Important colors include pale blue, cream, and gold.

Examples include Browning Plantation (ca. 1857 – 1858) in Chappell Hill, the McGregor-Grimm House (ca. 1861) at Winedale, and the Neese House (ca. 1872) in Warrenton. Similar in context, the House of the Seasons (ca. 1872) in Jefferson mixes Greek Revival and Victorian Italianate influences. Usually stencilling and freehand painting define frieze motifs, while graining and marbling embellish dados, doors, characterized by asymmetrical plans, irregular massing, uneven roof lines, ornamental woodwork, and decorative details. Continuity in exterior and interior design varied, but consistently reflected pattern upon pattern. Colors changed throughout the Victorian period, responding to popular revival influences as well as lighting improvements. Early schemes emphasized gold, rust, olive, gray, and cream, while the palettes of the early twentieth century incorporated paler tints and shades.

Unlike the traditional model, a number of examples in Texas reflected a diverse architectural language with structures varying from high style to vernacular and illustrating some ethnic influences. Architectural features were often abstracted, repositioned, and reinterpreted while classical wall divisions provided an ordered arrangement. Characteristic residential, religious, and commercial buildings with decorative painting are extant all over, but are better preserved (through love or financial constraints) in smaller communities. Some of the structures were decorated at the time of construction and some later. Victorian imagery predominates in all interiors, along with a distinct emphasis on stencilling and infill painting. Important colors include deep gold, olive, rust, brown, and cream. A significant number of structures date from the 1860s to the 1910s; the decorative painting is from the 1880s to the 1920s.

Victorian structures that accurately depict high style expressions are illustrated by the Walter Tips House (ca. 1876) in Austin, the Steves House (ca. 1876) in San Antonio, the Annunciation Catholic Church (ca. 1869, 1881) in Houston, the Walter Gresham House (ca. 1893, now called Bishop's Palace) in Galveston, the Border-Rudy House (ca. 1890s) in Galveston, and the Wilson House (ca. 1898) in Dallas. Decorative painting embellishes ceilings, walls (as an alternative to wallpaper), and floors. Common features include geometric ceiling designs with a perimeter border and a center medallion, upper walls with stencil patterns and a decorative frieze border, dados and doors with graining, marbling, or stencilling, and floors resembling decorative tiles or wood parquet.

In contrast, surviving rural buildings are often wood frame, late nineteenth-century vernacular farmhouses with a diverse selection of Victorian decorative painting. Examples include the Graves Homestead (ca. 1870s – 1880s) in Lilac community near Austin, the Marburger-Witte House (before ca. 1873, 1900) formerly in Shelby, the Sterrett House (ca. 1889, now destroyed) in Beckville, the Nordt-Dougherty House (ca. 1882) in Brenham, and the Dahse-Halla House (ca. 1880s – 1890s) in Weimar. Most of the decorative painting embellishes ceiling and walls, and common features imitate the high style examples. There is a strong German emphasis in the remaining vernacular examples.

Churches built during this period — many of them Catholic — imitated the Victorian Gothic Revival style and followed guidelines established nationally that defined the appropriate religious image. Of the numerous original examples with decorative painting, few retain their decorative appearance. The best existing buildings include St. Joseph's Catholic Church (ca. 1859) in Galveston and St. Mary's Catholic Church (ca. 1895) in Praha. Construction materials are either wood, brick, or stone depending on geographic location and available building supplies. Located primarily in communities settled by European immigrants, most churches also exhibit ethnic design characteristics, yet still illustrate numerous Victorian interpretations. Decorative painting usually embellishes ceilings and walls, and common features imitate high style examples.

Few examples of late nineteenth-century commercial structures with decorative painting remain in the state; those that do reveal diversity in style and character. Though substantially modified, they show a greater emphasis on stencilling. Very few artists are known by name, and of these, most are European immigrants.

The various structures represented here are typical as well as memorable illustrations of decorative painting. Some of the most unusual include the individual work of Rudolph Melchior at Winedale Historical Center near Round Top, European landscapes in the Gluck-Kadernoschka Place in Cat Spring, trompe l'oeil pictorial paintings in the Sterrett House in Beckville, fake perspective illustrated in the Wesley Brethren Church in Wesley, trompe l'oeil iron work in the First Presbyterian Church in Galveston, the grained portrait in the Addison-Gandy House in Montgomery, and the highly decorated floor in the Borden-Rudy House in Galveston. Each, in its own way, makes a unique contribution to the artistic heritage of Texas.

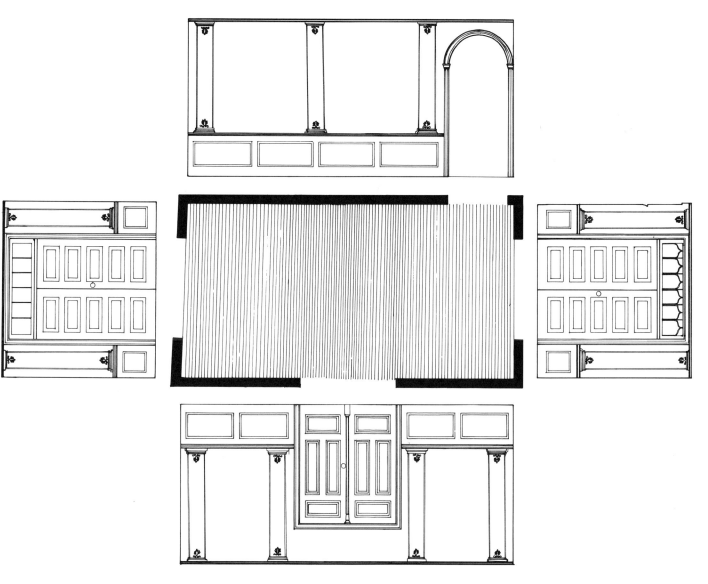

McGregor-Grimm House, Winedale

AREA: Entry Hall
SIZE: 9' – 11" wide × 19' – 5" long × 9' – 0" high
LOCATION: Walls
AREA: Parlor
SIZE: 18' – 2" wide × 19' – 1" long × 9' – 0" high
LOCATION: Ceiling
DECORATION: Stencilling, infill painting, freehand painting, graining
ARTIST: Rudolph Melchior
DATE: ca. 1861 – 1868
DRAWINGS: The University of Texas at Austin, Architectural Drawings Collection, Winedale Institute in Historic Preservation
DOCUMENTATION: Tina Howard Leva and Anne Moore

The McGregor-Grimm House (ca. 1861) illustrates a blend of fashions — the outgoing classical statement, the incoming Victorian style, and the German ethnic tradition. Vernacular in interpretation, the Greek Revival exterior envelops an interior displaying mixed influences. Originally in Wesley, now located at Winedale Historical Center, the house was built for C. G. McGregor and his wife. When Mr. McGregor died in 1862, he owned 1570 acres of land obtained from the Samuel May Williams league, thirteen slaves and property valued at $32,604. The house is decorated in five rooms. Research only reveals that the art was added sometime between the date of construction and the date of the artist's death.

The alleged German artist, Rudolph Melchior — who migrated to Texas in 1853 — came from a family of Prussian artists and resided in nearby Latium, Texas, a community of highly educated Germans. Following in the footsteps of his father, Mathias Andreas Melchior, Rudolph and his brother Ernst were established artists in Germany, designing stencils, painting houses, hanging wallpaper, and binding books. Rudolph married Sophie Menn on May 12, 1862. Sometime during 1867, Melchior went to Galveston to work and buy art supplies. He died there on January 14, 1868, of yellow fever.

Melchior's work in the McGregor-Grimm House closely matches the painting he did in the Lewis House, also now on the Winedale property in Round Top. The art depicts classical forms, planned balance, subdued color combinations, and curved floral patterns. The entry hall in particular displays many of these features. Melchior divided the walls into classical units through pilasters and dados, incorporated symmetrical balance, and used blue, white, and brown — all characteristic of the Greek Revival expression. The simple decoration, painted on wide horizontal wooden boards, blends with the architectural form. In the other spaces, the image is more Victorian and German. In the parlor, frieze and ceiling patterns feature multi-colored floral designs with vases holding fruits and flowers — symbolic motifs popularized in German trade journals and by the Peale family, noted portrait and still-life artists of the eighteenth and nineteenth centuries. Patterns are detached, band, and divider stencils positioned in typical Victorian layouts with perimeter borders on the walls or ceilings, where there are often center medallions. Although flatly rendered, the motifs offer a variety of colors.

Ceiling

Gluck-Kadernoschka Place, Cat Spring

AREA: Parlor
SIZE: 15' – 3" wide × 17' – 2" long × 9' – 8"
   high
SUBJECT: Old Texas State Capitol, Austin
AREA: Bedroom
SIZE: 14' – 9" wide × 16' – 9" long × 9' – 9"
   high
SUBJECT: European landscape
LOCATION: Walls
DECORATION: Freehand painting
DATE: ca. 1860s – 1880s

The earliest recorded example of freehand painting as individual ornamentation appeared in a small, wood-framed house known as the Gluck-Kadernoschka Place (ca. 1860s) in the Czech community of Cat Spring. Oral history indicates the original owner was probably saddlemaker Theo Gluck, but it is unclear how long he resided in this central Texas house. Deed records indicate John Hackbarth purchased the property in 1875, and a short while later moved the house a mile or so "down the road." In 1902, the Hess family acquired the residence, briefly renting it around 1920 to Mr. A. G. Kollatschny, who remem-

bers stars on the bedroom ceiling and an American eagle on the parlor ceiling. The Hesses subsequently sold the property in 1937 with fifty-one acres of land to Max Kadernoschka, a bachelor of Austrian descent. He had the art work painted over. As of this writing the fate of the house is unclear, and the murals have been removed so that they will be preserved.

Murals, originally on all walls, existed in two main rooms. In the parlor, the subject was a simplified version of the old Texas state capitol in Austin (ca. 1853 – 1881). The subject matter in the bedroom consisted of European landscape scenes resembling the river areas along the Swiss-Austrian border. Within the landscapes are mill sites, snow covered mountains, winding roads, and male figures. Analysis of the costumes indicates design details of the 1830s – 1860s, suggesting the Gluck family commissioned the decorative painting. All of the murals — painted on horizontal wooden boards above a dado area — are in shades of green, brown, blue, white, and gray. The landscape scenes imitate wallpaper, suggesting the desire for a more expensive type of decoration. Although the artist is unknown, oral history suggests an itinerant painter familiar with central Europe and with Texas history. Borrowing heavily from rural and ethnic traditions, this vernacular work shows little regard for popular national influences.

Knolle-Schroeder House, Industry

AREA: Parlor

SIZE: 17' – 2" long × 17' – 1" wide × 10' – 1" high

LOCATION: Wall

DECORATION: Stencilling, marbling (dado)

DATE: ca. 1860 – 1890s

DRAWINGS: The University of Texas at Austin, Architectural Drawings Collection, Winedale Institute in Historic Preservation

DOCUMENTATION: Mary Maier and Kathy Mensik

The town of Industry, founded in 1831 by Friedrich Ernst, is the cradle of German settlements. Initially located there and subsequently moved to Chappell Hill, the Knolle-Schroeder House (ca. 1868) contains stencil designs similar to those in the Jacomini farmhouse at Round Top and the Sieper-Knolle-Raeke House, built in Industry for Ernst's son-in-law, farmer Herman E. Knolle. A comparison indicates similar stylistic features by the same artist around the 1860s or 1890s. This house, built by J. Hahne and C. Schulze, has decorations in the parlor depicting Victorian floral and scroll patterns arranged in vertical stripes, equally spaced around the walls without regard for windows and doors. Band and divider stencils define the overall layout. Placed above a marbled dado area, the floral patterns were painted with several stencils, some inaccurately registered and blurred. Typical Victorian colors include a dull gray dado, a dull red upper wall, and patterns in gold, red, green, and blue. Resembling decorative Victorian wallpaper, the overall design suggests a depiction of current fashion executed by a person with limited capabilities.

St. Paul's Lutheran Church, Serbin

AREA: Nave
LOCATION: Columns
DECORATION: Marbling
ARTIST: August Weber
DATE: ca. 1871

St. Paul's Lutheran Church (ca. 1867 – 1871) is the religious seat of the only known Wend settlement in the United States. German in nationality and Slavic in language and culture, the Wends are descended from the Slavs of the Elbe River and Baltic coast. Considered foreigners by the Germans, they came to Texas to enjoy religious freedom. Their church attests to their marked individuality through its distinctive decoration. It is the third structure on the site, and measures 40' – 0" wide by 70' – 0" long by 24' – 0" high. Erected at a cost of $5000, it resembles the first minister's previous church in Kotitz, Germany. Following custom, women sat downstairs, and men in the balcony. According to local tradition, August Weber painted the interior around 1871. The "heavenly blue" ceiling has red stencil designs with "columns stained to look like marble." The marbling illustrates a feathering technique. Prominent leaf motifs — rendered in dark gray-green on a blue-gray background — are on all ten columns in the church. No other references have been found to describe why leaf motifs were used instead of vein lines common to marble, and no other building has been identified with this type of treatment.

Neese House, Warrenton

AREA: Bedroom
SIZE: 18' – 0" wide × 18' – 2" long × approx.
   10' – 6" high
LOCATION: Ceiling
DECORATION: Stencilling, freehand painting
ARTIST: Mathias Andreas Melchior
DATE: ca. 1870 – 1872
DRAWING: The University of Texas at Austin,
   Architectural Drawings Collection, Winedale
   Institute in Historic Preservation
DOCUMENTATION: Cynthia Blue and Tina Howard
   Leva

Located in Warrenton, the Neese House (ca. 1870 – 1872) exemplifies an individual German expression of decorative painting based on national models. Originally built by local carpenters for pros-

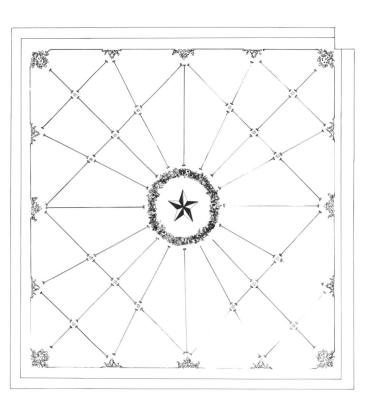

perous German business merchant William Neese, the house depicts the popular Greek Revival style as executed in stuccoed stone. Decoration in the ballroom and a bedroom conveys originality in details with attention to published layouts, but the character emphasizes the Victorian style rather than classical designs. Mathias Andreas Melchior, a German trained artist living in Round Top and father to Rudolph Melchior, ornamented the interiors using oilbase paints. Applied to a wood plank ceiling, the bedroom decoration features a center medallion composed of a flower wreath surrounding a German Bethlehem star similar to one in the Sterrett House in Beckville. From this composition, narrow radiating stripes end at stencilled anthemion shapes regularly spaced along the perimeter border. Motif colors are dull shades of red, gold, cream, and green applied on a pale blue-green ceiling. The layout is formal, but the effect is vernacular.

House of the Seasons, Jefferson

AREA: Dome
LOCATION: Cupola ceiling
DECORATION: Stencilling, infill painting, freehand painting
DATE: After ca. 1872

Located in Jefferson, the House of the Seasons (ca. 1872) contains an unusual domed cupola ceiling with high style decorative painting based on national models. Originally built for prosperous lawyer, politician, railroad president Benjamin Holland Epperson, the house is a blend of the Greek Revival and Victorian Italianate styles. Decoration on the dome ceiling conveys originality in details with attention to published formal layouts and classical designs. Applied to a plaster surface, the decoration features a center circle of geometric designs with trompe l'oeil panels shaped to the contour of the curve. In alternating sequence, the panels contain individualized classical figures representing the seasons and flanked on either side by others with a diagonal square grid. Colors are dull shades of gold, cream, and brown applied on a pale blue-gray ceiling.

Walter Tips House, Austin

AREA: Parlor
LOCATION: Ceiling
DECORATION: Stencilling, infill painting
DATE: After ca. 1876
PHOTOGRAPH: Austin Public Library
REPRODUCTION: Buie Harwood and Bill Kurtts,
 1974

The Victorian Italianate Walter Tips House (ca. 1876), built in Austin for a local German hardware merchant, reflects decoration based on national influences and published patterns. When first decorated, the ceilings in the four front rooms on the first floor were embellished with elaborate painting. Three rooms were covered over, however, with gypsum board in 1974, but the parlor was reproduced using fragments of the original painted work.

The original overall layout depicted high style models of Victorian taste. Resembling the work of Scottish designer George Ashdown Audsley, original ceilings typically had perimeter borders with a center medallion or a decorated field. The ornamentation depicted Victorian scroll and foliage patterns mixed with geometric motifs. In the entry, the repetitive designs recreated an oriental rug. In the front parlor, a perimeter border framed a large oval shape with elaborate details imitating acanthus leaf motifs placed in the corners. This motif repeated itself in the center

medallion. The overall composition combined detached, band, and divider stencils. Rendered in a water-base medium on plaster, the decoration illustrated an extensive twelve-color palette including dull and dark shades of green, red, gray, gold, and blue on a light ground. The effect was appropriate for the period as it represented the latest Texas fashion. The work was done by an unknown artist who must have had access to period books, catalogs, and trade journals.

Poe-Jones-Richardson House, Henderson

AREA: Parlor
LOCATION: Walls and ceiling
DECORATION: Stencilling, infill painting, freehand
 painting
ARTIST: Camile Montag
DATE: ca. 1870s

Located in Henderson, the Poe-Jones-Richardson House (ca. 1840s; destroyed by fire in 1982) displayed Greek Revival influences and the only known example of painted three-dimensional molding representing a binder stencil. Originally built for Dr. Winship S. Poe, a prominent North Carolina physician, the house increased in size with the 1870s Victorian addition for new owner James H. Jones, a distinguished Alabama lawyer. Each new section had painted interiors showing variety in architectural style but continuity in design. This suggests ornamentation applied after the Victorian addition. Camile Montag (1839 – 1912), a German-trained artist and interior decorator living in nearby Henderson, painted the interiors us-

ing hand-mixed oil paints. The parlor decoration was classical in concept, blending Greek Revival and Victorian Italianate characteristics. Particular features included classic wall divisions, ornate details, and a monochromatic color scheme. On the walls, painted rectangular panels shaped with binder stencils were integrated with decorative corner motifs defined by detached stencils. Applied on wood planks, the panels varied in size and showed little regard for architectural room divisions. These striped moldings and details continued on the ceiling area, accented by a classical medallion on the center axis. Colors were dull blue and gray with leaf motifs and striped bands spotlighted in shades of white.

Mission San Jose, San Antonio

AREA: Exterior facade
LOCATION: Walls
DECORATION: Stencilling, infill painting
ARTIST OF RENDERING: Ernst F. Schuchard
PHOTOGRAPH: The Library of the Daughters of
 the Republic of Texas at the Alamo, San
 Antonio

The red, yellow, and blue patterns on the front facade of Mission San Jose clearly suggest Moorish tile influences derived from the Spanish Alhambra and from Mexico. The simple interpretation may have been executed by missionaries, Indians, or regional artists. Decoration on the facade was apparently laid out with a rule and a compass.

As rendered by noted San Antonio scholar Ernst Schuchard, the mission looks very decorative. Conducting a survey of religious buildings during the 1930s and 1940s, Schuchard travelled from Texas to California to Mexico in search of historic artifacts. His meticulous notes, drawings, and documentation verify the existence of decorative art work in and on many mission buildings. By studying old photographs, he confirmed that decoration may have been applied to mission structures earlier than the 1860s and definitely before the 1890s. This is particularly true of several Texas missions. Reflecting a typical vernacular interpretation, Mission San Jose is characteristic of the mission history. Established in 1720 with the cornerstone laid in 1768, the church went through a series of mishaps in the nineteenth century. The church was restored extensively in 1934 and again in the 1970s.

Ernst Schuchard
1932

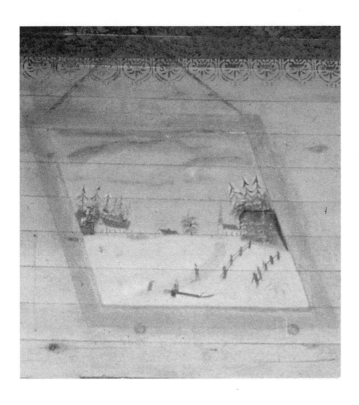

Sterrett House, Beckville

AREA: Parlor
LOCATION: Walls and Ceiling
DECORATION: Stencilling, freehand painting
SUBJECTS: Landscapes, probably from Germany
ARTIST: Itinerant painter
DATE: After ca. 1889 or 1890

The Sterrett House (ca. 1889; now destroyed) in Beckville, a rural community south of Longview, contained the only known example of trompe l'oeil Victorian picture frames. It was owned by Major Dowell Sterrett and his wife. An Alabama Civil War veteran, the major moved to Texas and established a medical practice. Originally containing several decorative rooms, this vernacular Victorian cottage had art work in the parlor — different landscape scenes placed within trompe l'oeil frames on wood planked walls. The parallelogram frames reflected the late nineteenth-century vogue of suspending paintings with the top edges floating from the surface. This ornamentation offered surprising vernacular subject variety, including the popular nineteenth-century painting *Winter in Maine*, a German landscape scene, the battle between the *Monitor* and the *Merrimac*, and a still life. Complementing this was a stencilled border cornice and a marbled dado. The simple decoration on the canvas ceiling consisted of a medallion with a German Bethlehem star and a floral wreath border. Colors varied from shades of gold and brown to blue and gray. Oral history holds that the work was executed by an itinerant painter around the time of construction. Such a portrayal of vernacular Victorian imagery is common in rural Texas.

Marburger-Witte House, Shelby

AREA: Parlor of the original "L" shaped house
SIZE: 16' – 0" wide × 17' – 0" long × 10' – 6" high
LOCATION: Ceiling
DECORATION: Stencilling
DATE: Before ca. 1900
DRAWING: The University of Texas at Austin, Architectural Drawings Collection, Winedale Institute in Historic Preservation
DOCUMENTATION: Barbara Redmon

Early wood-frame construction blended with Victorian style additions distinguishes the Marburger-Witte House, formerly in Shelby and now in Round

Top. Built for German Jacob Marburger and his wife, this simple vernacular structure was sold in 1872 to the Witte family. Painting is partially extant in two rooms of the original "L" plan structure. In the parlor, the wood board walls and ceiling illustrate simple decorative painting rendered in a precise technique. Visually the walls are separated into two colored sections — an upper area in dull pink and a dado area in grayed yellow. A repeating vine, depicted as a red and green band stencil, extends vertically along the wall corners and as a frieze motif. The cream-colored ceil-

ing has a decorative border composed of stripes, anthemions, and rinceau designs developed from detached, band, and divider stencils. A gradation of hue is typical. Colors vary in value from pale greens to medium blues to several shades of red, all popular during the late nineteenth century. The decoration sensitively relates to the home, using many of the motifs that appear in period trade catalogs and suggesting that the artist copied popular Victorian fashions.

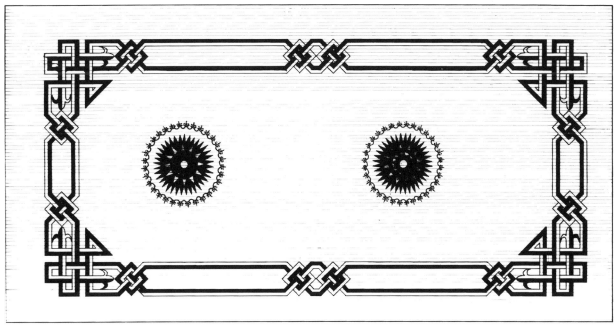

Ceiling

Wesley Brethren Church, Wesley

AREA: Nave
SIZE: 20' – 0" wide × 38' – 11" long × 13' – 4" high
LOCATION: Walls and ceiling
DECORATION: Stencilling, infill painting, freehand painting
ARTIST: Rev. B. E. Laciak
DATE: ca. 1889 – 1890
DRAWING: The University of Texas at Austin, Architectural Drawings Collection, Winedale Institute in Historic Preservation
DOCUMENTATION: Linda Flory

Wesley Brethren Church (ca. 1866, 1883), one of the smallest Texas churches, contains a unique trompe l'oeil interior with architectural features rendered in pre-Renaissance perspective concepts. Located in rural Wesley, Austin County, the one-room structure was built for Czech immigrants in a simple vernacular style expressing a folk tradition. It was decorated in 1889 and 1890 by the parish minister, Reverend Bohuslav Emil Laciak, who was accidentally killed in a hunting accident in 1891, leaving the project incomplete. The paintings represent an ordered classical style with Ionic columns on pedestals and a stylized perspective extending the space as side

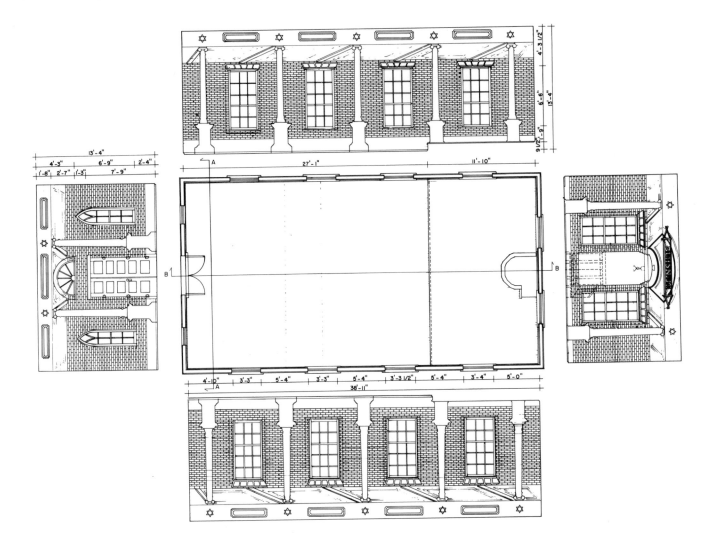

aisles. Similar in context to Moravian churches in central Europe, the perspective presents the viewpoint of the congregation rather than the minister at the pulpit.

The columns seem equally spaced around the perimeter edge with dark beams projecting from the capitals and extending to the false brick exterior walls, where the artist's pencil marks are still visible. The Czech word "busnami," meaning "God with Us," highlights art in the pulpit area, which was renovated in 1927. Martha Freeman writes in her monograph, *Wesley Brethren Church, Historic Structures Report*

(1980, p. 22): "Dr. T. S. Hruska attempted to rework the painted surfaces where the pulpit had formerly been situated, repainting the representations of brick work, and possibly lowering the painting of the chalice above the pulpit." The ceiling, composed of band and divider stencils, is more decorative with a geometric perimeter border and two stylized center medallions. The medium-value colors are shades of blue, brown, white, gray, and black. An engaging compositional aspect is the "folk" quality enhanced by small scale, ethnic features and Victorian character.

First Presbyterian Church, Galveston

AREA: Auditorium
SIZE: 4' – 2" high dado
LOCATION: Walls and ceiling
DECORATION: Infill painting, some stencilling
PATTERN SIZES: Scrolls — 3' – 0" wide
repeat × 2' – 8" high
DATE: ca. 1889

Completed at the same time as the Eiffel Tower, the First Presbyterian Church (ca. 1872 – 1889) in Galveston uniquely expresses a simple statement of late nineteenth-century fashion. It was designed by architect D. N. McKenzie in Norman Romanesque Revival style. The construction supervisor was Nicholas Clayton, who came from Memphis, Tennessee, to work on his first Texas project. George E. Dickey of Houston designed the interior at a cost of $10,000. The decorative artist is unknown. An article in *The Galveston Daily News* of February 1889 states "the walls are beautifully frescoed, and the harmonious blending of shades and colors is particularly pleasing to the eye." The impressive decoration was initially placed around the walls and on the ceiling, but only a small remnant remains above the dado and behind the organ. Here, large scroll shapes intertwine like ornamental iron work, a medium popular during the period. Significant in size, design, and placement, the stylized pattern is large, flat, and unique in the album of Texas decorative painting. It develops in shades of brown with gold on a beige background. Oil-base paint decoration adorns the plaster walls.

Addison-Gandy House, Montgomery

AREA: Bedroom
LOCATION: Door
DECORATION: Graining
DOOR SIZE: 2′ – 8″ wide × 6 – 9″ high
DATE: After ca. 1892

The Addison-Gandy House (ca. 1892) exemplifies an extensive use of graining in a Texas residence. Located in rural Montgomery near Conroe, the vernacular house is a wood-framed building commissioned by J. B. Addison and his wife Martha. Doors and mantels are grained in six rooms. Because of the extensive quantity, it is likely the work was executed shortly after construction. Records list several cabinetmakers working in the vicinity, and there are several 1890s structures with graining in the area. The anonymous artist was probably a local or itinerant painter. The interior doors resemble mahogany, but are distinguished by various grained panel treatments. The effects are feathered, burled, knotted, and streaked with straight and wavy long veins. No two panel treatments are alike. A portrait, highlighting a grained bedroom door panel, illustrates a well defined bearded face accented with a lighter color. The artist's style shows skill in oil-base paint application and a strong sense of individuality. Throughout the house, the graining appears without wallpaper or other types of decoration. This simplicity is common in turn-of-the-century buildings and indicates a shift from heavy Victorian ornamentation.

Annunciation Catholic Church, Houston

AREA: Apse
LOCATION: Ceiling
DECORATION: Freehand painting
SUBJECT: Transfiguration of Christ (Ascension mural)
DATE: ca. 1893

Popular religious subjects prior to the 1930s include mural representations of Christ's Ascension and show a central figure surrounded by angels and the apostles Peter, James, and John. This theme is realistically illustrated in Annunciation Catholic Church (ca. 1869, 1881) in Houston. The structure combines Romanesque, Gothic, Norman, and English exterior influences with an emphasis on interior Neoclassical detailing. Nicholas J. Clayton contributed to the influences during his architectural tenure from 1881 to 1884. The only area with decorative painting is the half-domed ceiling. According to church history, "the year 1893 saw the beautiful Transfiguration fresco placed over the main altar." This scene portrays the biblical passage: "And it came to pass, while he blessed them, he was parted from them, and carried up into heaven." The design is similar to one on the apse ceiling at Sacred Heart Catholic Church in Palestine, also a Clayton structure. The overall compositions are nearly identical, suggesting the work of the same unknown artist (the Palestine mural has been restored). The main difference is in the rendition of angels and cherubs — in Houston they are round and fat, but in Palestine they resemble 1930s portraits of young women. Both murals copy national influences, specifically the 1880s mural executed by famous American artist John LaFarge for Ascension Church in New York City.

St. Mary's Catholic Church, Praha

AREA: Nave and apse
LOCATION: Walls and ceiling
DECORATION: Stencilling, infill painting, freehand painting
ARTIST: Gottfried Flury
DATE: ca. 1895
PHOTOGRAPH: Texas Historical Commission, Austin, by Carol Kenedy and Linda Flory

St. Mary's Catholic Church (ca. 1895) in rural Praha, the Czech word for Prague, shows popular Gothic Revival features and displays European religious symbolism as interpreted by Czech immigrants. The simple stone and wood building contrasts with the richly ornamented interior. Embellished with work reminiscent of central European models, the trompe l'oeil paintings imitate ribbed vaults, Gothic tracery, religious images, and landscape scenes. At the church blessing, the November 28, 1895, *Southern Messenger* reported: "the ceiling is in keeping with the style and is richly decorated." Respected Texas artist Gottfried Flury (July 6, 1864 – October 29, 1936) is credited with the 1895 interior decoration.

Emigrating from Switzerland to New York City, Flury moved to Buffalo, St. Louis, and Kansas City before settling in central Texas in 1889. He advertised his services as a "scenic artist and fresco painter," and later painted signs in Austin. Various records indicate that he completed decorative projects for residential, religious, and commercial buildings in the towns of Flatonia, Hallettsville, Moulton, and Cestahowa. He resided in nearby Moulton while ornamenting the church interior at Praha. In her book *Our Father, Godfrey* (1976), daughter Dorothy Agnes Flury documents the work of her father in the building through records, interviews, and drawings. Having seen eight original drawings by her father, one depicting a group of angels like the image at Praha, this author was able to verify the same characteristic technique. The drawing of angels also matches one by Flury on view at the Institute of Texan Cultures in San Antonio.

On the interior wood-planked surfaces, two churches in Prague and three angels surrounding a cross dominate the central apse composition. The ceiling design incorporates trompe l'oeil ribbed vaults, Gothic capitals, and various religious symbols. Complementing this image, architectural panels with profuse plant life define the frieze area. The character follows traditional Gothic models for ecclesiastical structures, with some personal features added. The overall ceiling is a faded blue-green with decorative painting rendered in dull shades of blue, green, brown, gold, rust, and white.

Later additions were made in the apse area by resident priest and artist, Father Louis P. Netardus. Born in Moravia, he lived with his parents at Smothers Creek in Hallettsville and was appointed to the pastorate at Praha in 1901. He is supposed to have executed the painting of garlands on the lower apse wall, which is rendered in a decidedly different technique from that of Gottfried Flury.

*San Fernando Cathedral, San Antonio. (Courtesy Library
of the Daughters of the Republic of Texas at the Alamo, San
Antonio.)*

THREE

Variations: 1900 – 1925

Between 1900 and 1925, Texas designers endorsed national architectural trends, including complex variations in decorative painting. Texans continued to embrace Victorian styles but adopted new, popular national styles: the Arts and Crafts Movement, Art Nouveau, and the Colonial and Classical Revival. Many national styles reflected historic forms adapted for modern uses, blending past traditions with new technology. Most extant buildings illustrate this invasion of national and international ideas. Within this context, there is a mixture of residential, religious, and commercial structures, but most surviving examples are houses. These buildings can be found throughout the state, though they were mainly in towns served by the ever-expanding railroad system.

Railroads had a number of effects. They fostered growth in small towns and boosted development in larger metropolitan areas like Dallas, Fort Worth, Houston, and San Antonio. The rails not only carried new migrants from Europe and the other states, they also brought mass-produced goods from businesses such as Sears, Roebuck and Company, as well as books, magazines and services. The growing population of Texans — old and new — readily adapted to the influx of publications and products that now could be gotten with little delay and at far less expense. Building activity saw a sharp rise, particularly along new transportation routes leading north through the Panhandle, south to the Rio Grande Valley, and west to the deserts and mountains. Towns such as Wichita Falls, Amarillo, Harlingen, and El Paso attracted various ethnic nationalities, mixing together as a homogenous population.

Vernacular Victorian buildings continued to multiply throughout Texas during the early decades of the twentieth century, as testified to by numerous variations of surviving examples. The structures date primarily from the years of 1900 to 1915; decorative painting was most likely added within ten years of construction. Similar to others dotting the American landscape, the buildings resemble the simple, small, picturesque residential and religious edifices seen in Norman Rockwell paintings. Often copied — or even ordered — from catalogs like those of Sears, Roebuck and Company, the structures imitated past styles or borrowed from popular national styles. Extant examples with decorative painting are found mainly in rural areas like Brenham, Cistern, Lindenau, Fredericksburg, and Schulenburg. A few, however, remain in San Antonio. Many offer variations of stencilling, infill painting, freehand painting, and some graining or marbling. Decorative ornamentation was inspired by Victorian, Art Nouveau, Classical Revival, and other European influences. Color diversity is common, along with lighter values reflecting an interest in sanitary appearances and improved lighting conditions. But on the outside the buildings are often bland containers for interior embellishment.

Particularly good Victorian examples include Charles Martin Meister's work in Brenham, the Dieringer-Kuester-McChesney House (ca. 1900s) in Lindenau, St. Mary's Catholic Church (ca. 1905) in High Hill, and Ascension Church (ca. 1913) in Moravia. Wood is the primary building material for houses, and wood, stone, or brick were commonly used for churches. Since there is usually limited three-dimensional architectural delineation, the decorative painting — embellishing ceilings, walls (as an alternative to wallpaper), and floors — often defines and shapes the spaces. Classical divisions frequently divide wall areas with geometric panels providing an ordered arrangement for ceiling treatments. Copying earlier Victorian examples, typical interior features reflect prescribed layouts, decorative borders, and "pattern on pattern" ornamentation. These designs are more elaborate and better crafted, however, than earlier versions. Other unusual features illustrated in this group are rare stencilled floors and allover stencil decoration that imitates wallpaper.

English designers — William Morris, Phillip Webb, Edward Burne-Jones, Charles Robert Ashbee, and Walter Crane — influenced the growth of the American Arts and Crafts Movement around the turn of the century. This progressive school stressed simplicity, honest materials, handmade production, heavy structural features, and uncluttered environments. American advocates included Gustav Stickley, Frank Lloyd Wright, and Will Bradley, all widely published in consumer magazines like *Ladies Home Journal*. Their philosophy of simplifying design and planning for comfortable family living is reflected in Prairie, Craftsman, Bungalow, and Mission style buildings. Exterior and interior spaces called for informal, asymmetric, horizontal, and integrated concepts with open space, structural repetition, Japanese design, natural lighting, and attention to human scale. Rendered through stencilling or freehand painting, motifs often emulated the design character. Overall color selections and room hues were determined by the way interiors were oriented toward the sun. Dull values of brown, gold, cream, rust, and blue-green emphasized the popular image of a natural environment.

Numbering less than five, extant Arts and Crafts examples with interior ornamentation date to the first decade of the century with decorative painting added after construction. Excellent examples include the Warren-Crowell House (ca. 1903 – 1904) in Terrell, the Trost House (ca. 1906 – 1909) in El Paso, and the L. T. Wright House (ca. 1917) in San Antonio. Reflecting nationally recognized styles and integrated concepts, some were modelled after the Prairie image, while others blended Classical Revival influences with Prairie interpretations. Characteristic interiors had wood moldings, beamed ceilings, horizontal banding, built-in shelving, and decorative friezes. Incorporated as an ornamental element on the frieze and between or on ceiling beams, decorative painting displayed diversity with different designs in different spaces with different interpretations — a concept commonly advanced by design publications.

Paralleling craft developments, Art Nouveau emerged in stylish Paris and Brussels. Imperceptibly affecting architecture, the style firmly advocated a decorative character and rejected historicism. Conceived as a new and revolutionary concept, it emphasized design unity, symbolic meaning, natural curves, applied decoration, and asymmetry. Art Nouveau was international in scope with advocates in France and Belgium, as well as England, Scotland, and Germany. Important designers included Hector Guimard, Emil Galle, Henri van de Velde, Victor Horta, and Charles Rennie Mackintosh, whose strong, individual design theories filtered into the United States via books, magazines, and trade journals. American advocates and progressive interpreters included Louis Sullivan, Louis Comfort Tiffany, and James McNeill Whistler, each of whom developed unique conceptual variations. While selected exterior features were highlighted by various motifs, Art Nouveau interiors emphasized enriched surface treatments. Frieze motifs incorporated botanical forms, geometric repetitive patterns, decorative animals, and romantic figurative landscapes, all presented through stencilling and freehand painting. A symphony of color emphasized nature through hues of green, gold, brown, and dull red.

Art Nouveau seemed superficial and foreign to Texans, however. The concepts of the Arts and Crafts Movement better suited their rugged character. Consequently, very few Texas structures incorporated Art Nouveau decoration on the exterior or interior.

Surviving examples of Art Nouveau with interior ornamentation are in three locations: the Warren-Crowell House (ca. 1903 – 1904) in Terrell; the Bivins House (ca. 1904 – 1905) in Amarillo; and the Kruppa-Zimmerhanzel House (ca. 1910) in Cistern. Varying from high style to vernacular, all are different in size. Usually only one public space has Art Nouveau decoration while the other rooms display other stylistic influences. Curved line and floral patterns are similar, indicating close attention to international themes. The Kruppa-Zimmerhanzel house, which is representative of a group of similarly decorated buildings in Cistern, illustrates vernacular Art Nouveau interpretations based on Sears, Roebuck and Company stencil patterns. The collection of Cistern residences is distinctive because of pattern choice, house character, and ethnic heritage. Decorative painting in all the surviving examples dates from the first two decades of the century.

As interest in the classical styles faded, new approaches developed. One focused on Roman antiquity, resulting in the French Beaux Arts style. The other focused on eighteenth century French and American fashions popularized by internationally recognized decorator Elsie de Wolfe and resulted in the use of antiques and antique reproductions. In America, these concepts produced a myriad of revival style architecture and interiors from the 1900s to the 1940s. Following the tenets of architects Richard Morris Hunt and the firm of McKim, Mead, and White, buildings were dubbed Colonial or Classical Revival. Classical versions usually emphasized the temple form, while Colonial examples often imitated the Georgian form. Their exterior design utilized symbolism, light scale, large flat facades, and white exteriors. Strongly reflecting this design, interiors articulated classic wall divisions, depicted antique looks, and employed limited decorative painting on frieze or ceiling surfaces. Designs were derived from classical geometric compositions with motifs of figures, flowers, and swags. Period trade publications promoted particular decorative motifs for specific kinds of spaces and suggested pale colors of blue, gray, gold, green, and white.

This proliferation of classic design was nourished in American women's magazines, building catalogs, and by suburban developers, resulting in wide national popularity. Extant Colonial and Classical Revival buildings with interior ornamentation are limited in Texas, however. The scarcity may reflect a lack of national design acceptance, interior modification, or the availability of trained artists. Three good examples include the Wharton-Scott House (ca. 1903; now called Thistle Hill) in Fort Worth, the Burton-Merritt House (ca. 1905) in McKinney, and the Dilworth-Clemons House (ca. 1910) in Gonzales. Most residential examples are in high style structures built by wealthy owners. They represent diversity in location, scale, and influence. The result is a mixed selection of design motifs. Some are elaborate, others simple with interior decoration usually repeating the exterior character. Ornamentation includes classical motifs, naturalistic flowers, geometric patterns, and figurative compositions. The decoration — confined to interior wall and ceiling surfaces — is freehand or infill painting in gold, green, white, and blue with accents of rust.

Among these variations, selected examples are noteworthy for their high style character, while others are more memorable because of their vernacular image. Some of these include the decorative work by Charles Martin Meister in a collection of Brenham houses, the diversity of design in the Warren-Crowell House in Terrell, the painted flowers based on seed catalogs in the Harriman-Herlin House in Palacios, the allover stencilling resembling wallpaper in the collection of Lindenau houses, the elaborate decorative work in St. Mary's Catholic Church in High Hill, the European imagery created by Peter Plotkin for the Burton-Merritt House in McKinney, the Art Nouveau decoration in the Kruppa-Zimmerhanzel House in Cistern, the extensive selection of Donecker family work in central Texas, and the fish murals on the Champion Store and Restaurant facade in Port Isabel. It is significant to note that in some areas — Brenham and Lindenau, for instance — numerous buildings represent the work of a single artist who helped to leave a marked vernacular imprint on the state.

Dining Room Wall

Eichholt-Guderian-Kruse House, Brenham area

AREA: Dining Room
SIZE: 15′ – 3″ wide × 17′ – 3″ long × 9′ – 10″ high
LOCATION: Ceiling
AREA: Parlor (now a bedroom)
SIZE: 15′ – 3″ wide × 15′ – 6″ long × 9′ – 10″ high
LOCATION: Floor
PATTERN SIZE: 10″ wide × 10″ long squares
DECORATION: Stencilling, infill painting, freehand painting
ARTIST: Charles Martin Meister
DATE: ca. 1902
DRAWINGS: The University of Texas at Austin, Architectural Drawings Collection, Winedale Institute in Historic Preservation
DOCUMENTATION: Becky Hart and Sarah Brooks Eilers

The Eichholt-Guderian-Kruse House (ca. 1865; 1929) in Brenham is one of thirteen structures decorated by German artist Charles Martin Meister (February 4, 1875 – January 10, 1935). It was built for Henrich Eichholt, the first German settler in Washington County, and his wife Louise. Originally composed of four unornamented rooms, the vernacular wood-framed structure was embellished thirty-seven

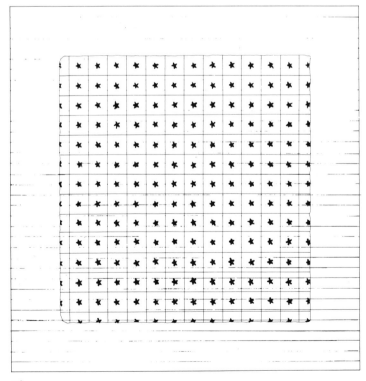

Floor

Eichholt-Guderian-Kruse House ceiling

years after initial construction. The house now contains a popular array of "pattern on pattern." Oral history indicates local artist Meister decorated all of the rooms. Having immigrated to the United States in 1891 to seek political refuge, Meister moved to Brenham around 1900. He was the only painter in town and worked by himself. Mixing his own liquid paints, Meister created elaborate, colorful, intricate, and personalized designs derived from Victorian images. Characteristic motifs include stylized anthemions, vines, fans, stars, fruits, flowers, baskets, birds, swans, and landscapes. Responding to lighter fashionable palettes, his decorations are in shades of cream, salmon, rust, blue, green, gray, and black. As a prime example of Meister's artistic work, this Brenham house maintains classic wall divisions and Victorian layouts. Interiors have grained dados, floral frieze borders, center medallions, and stylized perimeter borders applied to wood-planked surfaces.

In the dining room, an elaborately stencilled ceiling harmonizes with plainer walls framed by cornered pilaster silhouettes. Borders are detached band and divider stencils, integrated with a few individually rendered motifs. In the old parlor, there is a rare painted checkerboard floor with alternating stars. Complementing this, a personalized ceiling medallion depicts a small white bird holding a scroll containing the German phrase, "Welcome from the bottom of my heart, thy Father in Heaven rejoices in life." In the upstairs bedroom, the ceiling medallion contains a woman's portrait with a heart-shaped pin enclosing the letters "AB," possibly referring to Meister's daughter Hattie Anna Bertha. In the adjoining bedroom, a handwritten German phrase reads "I would have never done that thing myself." These unusual features characterize Meister's work.

Ceiling

Nordt-Dougherty House, Brenham area

AREA: Entry Hall

SIZE: 9' – 7" wide × 17' – 1" long × 11' – 6" high/dado 2' – 9" high

LOCATION: Walls and ceiling

DECORATION: Stencilling, infill painting, freehand painting

ARTIST: Charles Martin Meister

DATE: ca. 1900 – 1905

DRAWINGS: The University of Texas at Austin, Architectural Drawings Collection, Winedale Institute in Historic Preservation

DOCUMENTATION: Sally Parsley Condara

The Nordt-Dougherty House (ca. 1882) presents a pristine example of decoration reminiscent of turn-of-the-century wallpaper designs and also illustrates another project by Charles Martin Meister. Built near Brenham by either the Giese or the Nordt families, this wood farmhouse features decoration commissioned by German farmer William Nordt, uncle to Meister's wife. The exterior is plain, but the interior has two ornamented rooms left from the original six spaces. Similar in context to Meister's other work, the designs are fully detailed, well proportioned, and personally expressive. Applied on wood-planked ceilings and walls, the entry hall decoration captures Victorian imagery. An elaborate ceiling medallion with a perimeter border blends with a stylized floral frieze above a classically proportioned dado. Incorporating patterns from other projects, Meister imitated published stencil motifs and compositional layouts. Continuing this character, the dining room is more personal with distinctive corner motifs including a swan, a bird, a cornucopia, and a basket of flowers. Colors reflect a typical Meister palette.

This house indicates the way Meister received commissions, despite his lack of professional training and Brenham's small population. His first big project was the 1901 decoration of eight rooms in the C. H. Sander Mansion, where he fell in love with the owner's daughter Malinde and later married her.

Acquiring an instant contact base through marriage, as well as through the Lutheran church, Meister was hired to decorate some of the finest homes in this German farm community — mainly those of relatives or friends. They include the Jacob Folart House, the Engeling House, the Tegeler House, the Muegge-Winklemann House, the Winklemann House, the Quebe House, the Bockhorn Place, and the Schwettmann House.

Shortly after the birth of their only child, the Meisters moved to Houston where Charles went into business with Vincent Juenger, a fellow German decorator. Later he moved on to the Gulf Refining Company, where he continued to work until his death.

Wall

Wharton-Scott House (Thistle Hill), Fort Worth

AREA: Foyer Staircase
SIZE: 19′ – 11″ high × 22′ – 9″ wide × 16′ – 0″
  long/stencil, approximately 42″ high
LOCATION: Ceiling
DECORATION: Stencilling, infill painting
DATE: ca. 1903

A distinctive classical design imitating published national patterns distinguishes the decorative painting illustrated in the Wharton-Scott House, now called Thistle Hill (ca. 1903), in Fort Worth. According to tradition, the house was built by Texas cattle baron W. T. Waggoner for his only daughter Electra and her new husband Albert B. Wharton, Jr. Designed by the noted Fort Worth firm of Sanguinet and Staats, it initially imitated the Colonial Revival style. In 1912, it was modified to the Georgian Revival style by the same firm for the new owners, real estate magnate Winfield Scott and his wife Elizabeth. Reflecting a close design relationship between exterior and interior, the restored decoration embellishes walls of four public spaces. Some of the painting was commissioned by the Whartons and some by the Scotts.

In the symmetrically balanced staircase hall, stencilling adorns the plaster cove along the perimeter of the ceiling. Originally highlighting a gold wall, the decoration continues the character of the classic architecture and provides a harmonious design. Designed in an alternating sequence, the motifs imitate those found in the early twentieth-century trade catalogs like *Excelsior Stencils* from Chicago and *Alabastine Stencils* from Grand Rapids. Stylized in depiction, they show ionic volutes, acanthus leaves, classical vases, and anthemion motifs ordered by the alternating axis of circles, squares, and rectangles. Value changes create shading for the dominant colors of green and rust on a pale gold background. Although unknown, the artist definitely used trade catalogs and journals to create a sophisticated classical image for the client.

Dining Room Wall

Warren-Crowell House, Terrell

AREA: Parlor-Sitting Room
SIZE: 15' – 6" wide × 16' – 7" long × 10' – 0"
   high
LOCATION: Walls (frieze)
AREA: Dining Room
SIZE: 14' – 10" wide × 24' – 5" long × 10' – 0"
   high
LOCATION: Walls (above wainscot)
DECORATION: Stencilling, infill painting
ARTIST: Keith and Company
DATE: ca. 1904

An extensive and varied stencil collection is extant
in the Warren-Crowell House (ca. 1903 – 1904) in
Terrell east of Dallas. The house was designed by
noted Dallas architect James Edward Flanders, who
blended high style Colonial Revival and Prairie
school influences. It was built for Robert and Annie
Warren with newly acquired Spindletop oil money.
Integrated with the exterior design are six interior
rooms that reflect turn-of-the-century fashion. Each
room is decorated differently. The ornamentation
was completed by the Kansas City firm of Keith and
Company over a six-week period. The spaces demonstrate individuality, sophistication, taste, and wealth.

In the combination parlor and sitting room, two
interwoven geometric curved patterns compose a

Parlor Wall

frieze strongly imitating Louis Sullivan's design work with patterns in greens, blues, browns, and golds. In the dining room, the Art Nouveau wall decoration has floral patterns with stripes and swirls rendered in blue-greens, pinks, yellows, and white. In the music room, the coved frieze decoration presents a subdued French Rococo character combined with classical motifs, all depicted in colors of beige, dull green, and peach. Other rooms with painted decoration demonstrate this same variety. It was common during this period to decorate areas with different themes, following specified rules in trade journals. Embellished spaces were often designated as masculine or feminine through style, line, and color.

Close examination of design layouts in the Warren-Crowell House indicates meticulous attention given to pattern placement by centering and spacing motifs aligned with interior architectural features. This, coupled with a well-executed artistic technique, identifies high-quality work. Oil-base paints, generally applied on canvas, appear throughout.

Bivins House, Amarillo

AREA: Parlor
SIZE: 19′ – 6″ wide × 22′ – 10″ long × 11′ – 0″ high
LOCATION: Walls and ceiling
DECORATION: Stencilling, infill painting, freehand painting
DATE: ca. 1905

The Bivins House (ca. 1904 – 1905) in Amarillo typifies the Panhandle image of a prominent cattle rancher and oil developer. Depicting the Colonial Revival architectural expression, it was built for Lee Bivins (October 7, 1862 – January, 1929) and his wife Mary Elizabeth Gilbert. Bivins moved to Amarillo in 1890 and went into the cattle business. Mrs. Bivins followed from Grayson County with their children in 1902. In time he owned 500,000 acres of grazing land stocked with cattle that he bought in Kansas City and other Midwest trading centers. In an unpublished paper ("Voices from the Past"), researcher James Allen states that "he was the largest landowner in the western half of the United States, and was known as the largest individual cattleman in the world." Oil and gas were found on his property in 1918, further assuring his wealth.

Four rooms display patterns with diverse aesthetic treatments such as Art Nouveau motifs, European landscape scenes, and Italian Renaissance Revival designs — all in harmony with the architectural features. This transitional image mixing, also seen in the Warren-Crowell House, was common during the time. The parlor frieze (restored) has circular medallions containing European landscapes and geometric Art Nouveau scroll motifs placed in alternating sequence. The overmantel continues the design with scrolls and a stylized classical vase. Emphasizing shades and values, colors are gold, blue, and pale green. Mrs. Bivins entertained frequently and the couple travelled often, accounting for the high style decorative concept.

Harriman-Herlin House, Palacios

AREA: Upstairs Bedroom
SIZE: 12' – 0" wide × 13' – 0" long × 10' – 3" high
LOCATION: Ceiling
AREA: Parlor
SIZE: 14' – 0" wide × 15' – 6" long × 10' – 0" high
LOCATION: Ceiling
SUBJECT: From seed catalogs
DECORATION: Stencilling, infill painting, freehand painting
Artists: Mr. Russell and Mr. Ballard
DATE: ca. 1905

The Harriman-Herlin House (ca. 1905 – 1910) in Palacios exhibits a realistic and stylized collection of painted flowers derived from seed and stencil catalogs. Built for the Harriman family, who were originally from Nebraska, this early twentieth-century vernacular two-story, wood-frame house contains decorative painting in seven rooms (some partially restored). Rendered in oil-base paint on either a canvas or plaster surface, the flowers reflect design diversity. Since flowers are plentiful along the Gulf Coast, it is probable the Harrimans enjoyed a typical Victorian rose garden — popular period flowers and the species that predominantly decorates the house. Oral tradition holds that two artists worked on the house at different times — first a Mr. Russell, then a Mr. Ballard. This is probably accurate since the flowers are painted in two techniques. Of particular significance, the scroll and anthemion motifs painted in an upstairs bedroom by Russell match 1907 patterns in Lindenau executed by Gustav Luerssen, indicating the same stencil catalog. Arranged in popular fashion, a geometric shape such as an oval, square, or rectangle orders the decoration, with placement either on the ceiling or coved frieze. Colors and their applications vary extensively, ranging from shades of dull green to red, brown, gold, white, and blue.

Parlor

Bedroom

Dieringer-Kuester-McChesney House, Lindenau

AREA: Entry Hall
SIZE: 9' – 11" wide × 15' – 1" long × 11' – 7" high
LOCATION: Walls, ceiling, floor
DECORATION: Stencilling, infill painting, graining, marbling (dado)
ARTIST: Gustav Luerssen
DATE: ca. 1910
PHOTOGRAPH: Mary Helen Pratte

In the small German farm community of Lindenau, southeast of San Antonio near Cuero, is an extensive collection of vernacular decorative painting executed by Swedish immigrant Gustav Luerssen (January 19, 1859 – December 30, 1937). Noteworthy for their similar designs, color palettes, classical motifs, and wallpaper effects, these houses illustrate a vivid interpretation of Victorian "pattern on pattern." Dating to the early 1900s, when about 200 people lived in Lindenau, the collection of wood-frame buildings includes the Dieringer-Kuester-McChesney House (ca. 1910; originally owned by Jacob and Veronika Dieringer), Boehm House (originally owned by Joseph and Emelia Boehm), Kahlich House (originally owned by Roudolf and Franziska Kahlich), Charlie Schlenstad House (destroyed), John Arndt House (destroyed), August Ollie House (destroyed), and St. Johns Evangelical Lutheran Church (painted over). Many original owners were cotton farmers. They were Lutheran and related by blood or marriage. Immigrating from the same German-Austrian area, they developed communal living patterns consistent with those of their mother country. Since the railroad bypassed the community in 1906, these rural ethnic patterns continued undisturbed. The isolation of this little community is demonstrated by the lack of electricity until the late 1930s.

In Lindenau, Brenham, Cistern, San Antonio, and several other Texas communities, rural settlers frequently commissioned the same decorative painter for all interior work. In this instance they chose professional painter Gustav Luerssen, who lived in Westhoff (seven miles west of Lindenau) with his wife Sophie. Working by himself, Luerssen mixed his own oil-base paints and followed established period examples.

Consistent from one structure to another, colors include shades of gray, rust, pink, blue, green, and brown. Repeated classical motifs are anthemion, scroll, rinceau, guilloche, and acanthus leaves. Rare

examples of allover stencilling resembling wallpaper are extant in the parlors and halls of the three remaining houses. The stencilled checkerboard parlor floor in the Dieringer-Kuester-McChesney house is also rare. All of the decoration is on wood planked surfaces, but the quality varies even though it conforms to published styles. Uniform in appearance, the graining imitates a straight grain walnut cut copied from national trade publications. The marbled dado, usually found below the allover stencilling, imitates jasper marble, but it is not a textbook example. Except for this quality flaw, few ethnic features are evident in the houses, suggesting that Luerssen was giving the owners a taste of high style rather than a pictorial European legacy.

Dilworth-Clemons House, Gonzales

AREA: Master Bedroom
SIZE: 15′ – 0″ wide × 29′ – 7″ long × 12′ – 0″
  high
LOCATION: Walls (frieze)
DECORATION: Infill painting, freehand painting
SUBJECT: A variety of different flowers (14
  compositions total)
Subject Sizes: 2′ – 2″ wide × 1′ – 3″ high
ARTIST: Unknown artist from Vienna
DATE: ca. 1910-1920

The Dilworth-Clemons House (ca. 1910) in
Gonzales contains an extensive collection of painted
flowers derived from seed catalogs and popular gar-
dening publications. The Classical Revival structure,
built for prominent banker Robert Scott Dilworth and
his wife, is ornamented in two bedrooms. Probably
decorated prior to 1920, ceilings and frieze areas contain a wide variety of floral motifs. Light and delicate
in appearance, these vary from roses and daisies to
dogwood and chrysanthemums. Rendered in pastel
shades of pink, yellow, white, blue, and green on
either a pale gray or blue background, the colors show
a strong relationship to the architectural style. Design
placement by an unknown Viennese artist shows evidence of attention to scale, spacing, and architectural features.

Browning Plantation, Chappell Hill

AREA: Southwest Bedroom
SIZE: 19′ – 6″ wide × 19′ – 9″ long × 11′ – 9″
  high
LOCATION: Doors, cornice, molding
DECORATION: Graining
DATE: ca. 1910 (restored or painted over)
DRAWING: The University of Texas at Austin,
  Architectural Drawings Collection, Winedale
  Institute in Historic Preservation (by Bill
  Blodgett)
DOCUMENTATION: Catherine Suttle

Browning Plantation (ca. 1857 – 1858) in Chappell Hill near Brenham is one of a few Greek Revival
structures with extant decorative painting. Added almost fifty years after initial construction, the decoration embellishes elaborately carved architectural features. Originally built at a cost of $2600, the house
was home to prominent civic leader and college president William W. Browning and his wife Elizabeth.
He held vast agricultural interests valued at $141,000
in 1860 and owned sixty-seven slaves, 600 cattle, and
over 2000 acres of land.
  The building maintains a typical, stylistic symmetrical plan with four rooms and a central hall on both
the first and second floors. Inside, beautifully carved
window and door moldings were left unornamented
until 1910. At this time, the house was owned by the
D. H. Matthew family, who commissioned an artist
to grain many of the moldings as well as mantels.
Imitating a straight cut, the medium brown walnut
graining, accented with repetitive spots of gold, appears uniformly well executed. Graining on the man-

tels differs, however, varying in application and wood type. Typical woods include mahogany and walnut, as well as others copied from samples in trade publications. Overall, the graining is more individualistic than textbook examples.

St. Mary's Catholic Church, High Hill

AREA: Nave and sanctuary
LOCATION: Walls, ceiling, columns (marbling)
DECORATION: Stencilling, infill painting, freehand painting, marbling
ARTISTS: Ferdinand Stockert and Herman Kern
DATE: ca. 1912
PHOTOGRAPH: Texas Historical Commission, Austin by Carol Kennedy and Linda Flory
DRAWING: Leo M. J. Diehlmann of St. Mary's Catholic Church at High Hill. It represents a typical design for many of his churches. Drawing courtesy of the Diehlmann Collection, Library of the Daughters of the Republic of Texas at the Alamo, San Antonio.

St. Mary's Catholic Church (ca. 1905 – 1906) in High Hill near Schulenburg is a big city church in a small town. Built for German and Czech Moravian settlers, its central European designs reflect the heritage of the worshippers and of the artists. Many of the designs resemble those found along the Rhine River in Germany, Switzerland, Austria and Czechoslovakia, as well as those of the English Arts and Crafts Movement. Incorporating the fashionable Gothic Revival style, the building is an excellent example of work by noted San Antonio architect Leo M. J. Diehlmann.

Of German heritage and Catholic persuasion, Diehlmann practiced primarily in the ethnic enclaves of central Texas and completed a significant number of Catholic churches with decorative painting. His designs include St. John the Baptist Church in Ammansville, Church of the Guardian Angel in Wallis (restored), St. Mary's Catholic Church in Fredericksburg, Our Lady of Grace Catholic Church in Lacoste (painted over), St. Sophia Greek Orthodox Church in San Antonio, Sacred Heart Church in San Antonio (destroyed), Nativity of the Blessed Virgin Mary Parish Church in Cestahowa (painted over), Our Lady of Lourdes Parish Church in Victoria (status unknown), Our Lady of the Lake Chapel in San Antonio, St. Cyril and Methodius Church in Dubina (painted over), and St. Joseph's Catholic Church in San Antonio (1912 addition).

Having collaborated with Diehlmann on previous projects, Germans Ferdinand Stockert (December 31, 1874 – February 2, 1940) and Herman Kern were "engaged to beautify the entire interior" of the High Hill church in 1912. Trained in Germany, Spain, and Russia, Stockert migrated to San Antonio in 1908 with his German wife Mary Elizabeth Flocke. Of

their four sons, only Fred worked briefly with his father in 1916. Youngest son Herman indicates his father decorated several buildings in San Antonio including the Lutcher-Brown House, the San Fernando Cathedral, the Municipal Auditorium, Our Lady of the Lake Chapel, and his own house on Hackberry Street, as well as St. Mary's Catholic Church in Fredericksburg and a small church in Honey Creek near Boerne.

Bachelor Herman Kern worked with Stockert in 1909 at the Fred Hummert Company, an art- and paper-hanging supply firm in San Antonio. In 1911, they were in business together as "painters and decorators." St. Mary's is one of their early projects. Kern boarded with Stockert some until 1918, when he apparently returned to Europe. Stockert resided in San Antonio until his death. In comparing the inventory of work by Stockert and Kern to that by Diehlmann, it is apparent the collaborative relationship was maintained for a long time.

According to oral history, pattern designs in the church are from books in Stockert's library. The stencils were cut by hand. Freehand and infill painting on ceiling and walls in the nave, sanctuary, and foyer illustrate Gothic rib vaulting and German ornamental foliage. Religious symbols positioned along the side aisles incorporate grapes and wheat (Holy Communion), a pelican (Atonement), a fleur de lis (Virgin Mary and the Holy Trinity), and a star made of two triangles (Holy Trinity). In the apse spandrel, two angels with the words "Santus, Santus, Santus" (meaning holy, holy, holy, or sacred) flank a crouching lamb. Lead-base colors are greens, pale blue, gold, and dull red on a cream wood planked surface.

Complementing this and framing the center aisle, ten reddish-brown columns simulate sienna marble. Uniform in appearance, each column has distinctive black and white, rope-like lines placed on an irregular diagonal grid. Completing the overall effect, the painted baseboards are gray and white and resemble dove marble. An impressive decorative product, this interior strongly blends painting with architectural form — an important quality in good design.

Burton-Merritt House, McKinney

AREA: Entry
LOCATION: Walls and ceiling
SUBJECT: Draped woman with cherubs
AREA: Parlor
SIZE: 15′ – 0″ wide × 17′ – 0″ long × 10′ – 0″ high; frieze 1′ – 6″ high
LOCATION: Walls and ceiling
SUBJECT: English allegory after Odilon Redon
DECORATION: Stencilling, infill painting, freehand painting
ARTIST: Peter Plotkin
DATE: ca. 1912–1915
PHOTOGRAPH: Dan Hatzenbuehler

The Burton-Merritt House (ca. 1905) in McKinney contains fashionable, diverse, and unique examples of freehand painting. It is one of the most engaging collections in the state because the decoration closely relates to art history models from well-known European and American artists. Rendered in a sophisticated manner, extant decorative paintings represent different characters and different periods. Built in 1905 for Dr. Ben Throckmorton, son of a Texas governor, the house was sold three years later to prominent medical specialist Dr. Edwin L. Burton. He commissioned Italian artist Peter Plotkin to decorate the interior sometime between 1912 and 1915, after seeing the artist's work on display in Italy and in New York City. Plotkin, who worked on the project for nine months, lived in the hotel next door.

The artist imitated European and American subjects as he decorated five rooms in the house. Copying eighteenth century French Rococo designs from Antoine Watteau, the entry ceiling depicts a partially draped female surrounded by cupids floating in a romantic landscape. Copying a romantic English allegory, the parlor ceiling imitates the work of symbolist dream painter Odilon Redon. The illustration combines a late-nineteenth-century style angel with a genteel turn-of-the-century woman. Garlands of flowers provide the frieze border pattern in colors of browns and blues.

Equally well ornamented, the library ceiling imitates the 1886 allegorical painting *Hope* by English artist George Frederick Watts. In the painting, a woman sits blindfolded on a globe and holds a lyre. This decoration reflects the same color scheme as the parlor. Departing from romantic imagery, the dining room walls show hunting scenes, including a variety of realistic birds and animals, much like the works of naturalist painter John James Audubon. Burton ap-

parently requested this subject matter, as he was fond of hunting on a nearby lake, but the placement of hunting scenes in a dining space was contrary to all trade publication rules.

Plotkin signed his work in the library and used the initials "RRA" after his name, possibly indicating registered membership in the English Royal Academy. Executed in oil-base paints on canvas, decorations in this house show excellent craftsmanship by a knowledgeable artist with high style taste.

Kruppa-Zimmerhanzel House, Cistern

AREA: Parlor

SIZE: 15′ – 4″ wide × 15′ – 4″ long × 9′ – 0″ high

LOCATION: Walls and ceiling

DECORATION: Stencilling, infill painting, freehand painting

ARTIST: Czech painter

DATE: ca. 1912–1915

PHOTOGRAPHS: Mary Helen Pratte and Buie Harwood

SEARS, ROEBUCK AND COMPANY STENCIL PATTERNS: These patterns were published in the Sereco Paint Catalog in 1911 and for several years following.

Located in the Czech community of Cistern south of Smithville, the Kruppa-Zimmerhanzel House (ca. 1910; originally owned by Frank and Annie Kruppa) contains the only known examples of Sears, Roebuck and Company stencil patterns in Texas. Allegedly a Czech painter worked on the structure, which is part

of a collection of buildings decorated between 1912 and 1915. Other wood-frame buildings include the Tomecek-Beck House (originally owned by Frank and Emelia Tomecek), the Mares House (originally owned by Joseph and Matilda Mares), the Psencik House (partially painted over; originally owned by Adolph and Rose Psencik), and St. Cyril and Methodius Catholic Church (painted over).

As a group, the houses include the same stencil patterns, freehand designs, and compositional arrangements. Using popular, mass-produced Art Nouveau designs from the "Sereco Paint Catalog" of 1911, an itinerant artist selected brown stencil plates varying in price from twenty-four cents to ninety-six cents each. Oral tradition holds that the artist was a fifty-year-old bachelor who drank a lot. He stayed in the area two years, boarding with owners, then returned to Moravia, Czechoslovakia. Incorporating a skilled technique, he executed ceiling medallions by hand, using postcards for inspiration. Colors vary from one house to another but maintain harmony through medium values.

St. Peter's Catholic Church, Lindsay

AREA: Nave and apse

LOCATION: Walls and ceiling

DECORATION: Stencilling, infill painting, freehand painting

SUBJECTS: Romanesque character with religious figures and symbols

ARTISTS: Friedolin Fuchs, Mathias Zell

DATE: ca. 1919

PHOTOGRAPH: Texas Historical Commission, Austin, by Carol Kennedy and Linda Flory

St. Peter's Catholic Church (ca. 1918) in the German farm community of Lindsay presents an elaborate and extensive collection of Romanesque and Byzantine trompe l'oeil decoration. As reported in the *Southern Messenger* at the 1919 dedication, the building was "designed by Mr. Frank Ludewig, an architect from Holland, at present living in St. Louis, Missouri. The decorations, which are in harmony with the style of the structure, were designed by Mr. Ludewig and executed by Mr. F. [Friedolin] Fuchs of St. Louis, Missouri, who in 1914 decorated the old church." Swiss artist Fuchs decorated a St. Louis church, and later the Benedictine Abbey in Subiaco, Arkansas, before coming to Lindsay. Interiors in this Texas church display dressed masonry walls in rust, brown, beige, and gray, interspersed with medieval manuscript patterns. Ceilings ornamented with circles, stars, and crosses mirror the variety of colors. Six panels depicting St. Boniface, the patron saint of Germany, and St. Benedict, the founder of the Benedictine order, were subsequently added by Dr. Mathias Zell, father of former pastor Reverend Bernard Zell.

St. John the Baptist Church, Ammansville

AREA: Nave
LOCATION: Walls and ceiling
DECORATION: Stencilling, infill painting, marbling
ARTIST: Donecker and Sons
DATE: ca. 1919
PHOTOGRAPH: Texas Historical Commission

St. John the Baptist Church (ca. 1919) in Ammansville contains the oldest complete example of decoration by the only known family of Texas painters. Built for Czech cotton farmers, it is one of seven churches and sixteen structures decorated between 1904 and 1947 by German artist Fred Donecker (March 23, 1860 – January 6, 1928) and sons William (February 26, 1886 – October 21, 1972) and Herbert (August 8, 1895 – April 6, 1957), and grandson Leo, all of San Antonio. Fred emigrated from Weisbaden with his wife Mary and worked in St. Louis, Chicago, Denver, and Kansas before relocating to Texas in 1900, where he decorated the W. T.

Waggoner Mansion (El Castile) in Decatur. Several years later, he moved to the San Antonio area, billing himself frequently in the *Southern Messenger* as a "fresco artist, church decorating a specialty." The Ammansville church is one example of the family's decorative repertoire, which also includes Catholic churches in Fredericksburg, Sweet Home, Moravia, New Braunfels, Castroville, and Lacoste — the latter two having been painted twice by the Doneckers.

Designed in the Gothic Revival style by architect and builder John Bujnoch, the exterior conveys an important image for the rural Catholic community and exemplifies the accepted national style for religious projects. The decorative interior emphasizes educational motifs, with distinctive ornate patterns including garlands, scrolls, foliage forms, palm fronds, and interlocking circles — all typical Donecker motifs. An unusual combination of pink, green, and white decoration entirely covers the ceiling and walls. Divided into rectilinear panels, the composition integrates well with the architectural features — evidence of high quality craftsmanship and meticulous handling of oil-base paints on a canvas surface.

L. T. Wright House, San Antonio

AREA: Living Room
LOCATION: Walls
DECORATION: Stencilling, infill painting, freehand painting
ARTIST: Donecker and Sons
DATE: 1917 – 1920
PHOTOGRAPH: Catherine Suttle

The Prairie style Lawrence T. Wright House (ca. 1917), designed by noted San Antonio architect George Willis, emulates work of nationally known architect Frank Lloyd Wright. Built for a local contractor, it has interiors with low beamed ceilings, wide frieze panels, and integrated open spaces. From 1917 to 1920, Fred Donecker and his sons embellished the entry, living room, and dining room. Reflecting the Arts and Crafts character, the living room boasts geometric ceiling and dado designs complemented by a naturalistic frieze border composed of vases, flowers, scrolls, and foliage. Upper wall areas incorporate scenic murals depicting local scenes, such as the sunken gardens, a seascape with Bolivar lighthouse, Brackenridge Park, a San Antonio mission, and a dancing scene. Signed "Fred Donecker and Sons, 1920," the art varies in color but emphasizes gold, brown, cream, green, and blue — typical Donecker selections.

Similar decorative features appear in the dining room but show strong functional design. These frieze motifs include garlands of five-pointed leaves — another Donecker signature — and still-life compositions of cornucopia and fowl, subjects prescribed in the trade publications for this type of space. Repre-senting an important time in the Doneckers' development, this house presents a well-coordinated design statement.

Burg-Donecker-Mahalia House, San Antonio

AREA: Dining Room
SIZE: 16′ – 2″ wide × 17′ – 9″ long × 11′ – 11″ high; frieze 2′ – 1″ high
LOCATION: Walls and ceiling
DECORATION: Stencilling, infill painting, freehand painting
ARTIST: Donecker and Sons
DATE: ca. 1922
PHOTOGRAPH: Mary Helen Pratte

The Burg-Donecker-Mahalia House (ca. 1890s) in San Antonio has five rooms ornamented by Fred Donecker and his family. Originally built for prominent city physician Sid Burg, the house became the Donecker residence around 1922. As such, it represents one of their five personally owned homes that they decorated in San Antonio over a forty-year period. The others include residences on Cherry Street, Montana Street, and in Madonna as well as the Donecker-Hadley House. In many of these houses, the artists repeated the same motifs used in churches, including a spider web, interlocking circles, vases, scrolls, and flowered garlands.

The Burg-Donecker-Mahalia House is simple and classical on the exterior, but the interior includes an expressive range of Donecker work. In the dining

room, ceiling decoration incorporates four classical vases holding white flowers surrounded by scroll and foliage forms, all positioned on four center axes and rendered with infill and freehand painting. Framing the design, a spider web border aligns with a frieze composed of delicate flower garlands. The Doneckers maintained their typical palette of rose, green, blue, gold, and cream throughout the composition — all fashionable Colonial Revival colors. One peculiar addition to the space is the inclusion of a still life easel painting of realistic fruits, vegetables, and household containers placed on a table. Attached to an upper wall, it is signed "William Donecker, 6/2/12" — obviously executed prior to building ownership. Except for this addition, the overall composition imitates wallpaper and borrows heavily from period trade publications. Decoration is also extant in the living room, entry, and stair hall, the latter boasting another easel painting of a young girl in Greek attire in a fantasy-like environment. It is signed "Fred Donecker 1904."

Many of the effects created in this house are also evident in the Steves House — built for lumber baron Ed Steves in 1876 — in the King William historic area. Son Albert possibly had five rooms decorated by the Doneckers sometime between 1910 and 1920. The Donecker style is particularly noticeable in the parlor where the trademark garland with five-pointed stars appears.

Ascension Church, Moravia

AREA: Apse
LOCATION: Walls and ceilings
DECORATION: Stencilling, infill painting, freehand
    painting
SUBJECT: Ascension of Christ
ARTIST: Donecker and Sons
DATE: ca. 1923
PHOTOGRAPH: Texas Historical Commission

Ascension Church (ca. 1912 – 1913) in Moravia presents a typical expression of church decoration by Donecker and Sons. Designed by the parish minister,

Father Schindler, and built by contractors Koch and Sons of Flatonia, it is a simple Gothic style building constructed for Czech Moravian settlers. Located in a small rural community similar to Ammansville, the structure is a distinctive presence on the landscape. According to church history, the inside was painted in 1923 by Donecker and Sons at a cost of $2000.

The interior apse walls, extensively covered with trompe l'oeil decoration, illustrate the Ascension of Christ into Heaven against a backdrop of clouds and angels. Pilasters and corinthian capitals frame the composition. This educational and symbolic design, strongly reminiscent of work by New York muralist John LaFarge, also appears in the church at Sweet

Home. Other wood-planked walls are ornamented in brown and gold to match stone blocks, complemented with rinceau borders, flower garlands, and palm fronds. The latter motif was featured in many popular trade catalogs, including one published by H. H. Birge and Sons in 1885. The ceiling, also decorative, has repetitive medallions containing a variety of religious symbols such as a chalice (Holy Sacrament), an open Bible (word of God), a reclining lamb (the Revelation), and two crosses. Colors emphasize shades of blue, white, gold, and brown — a typical Donecker palette.

One other characteristic Donecker motif appearing in select churches is a geometric tile design, usually in blue, gold, and burgundy. Probably a later trademark of son William, it was featured, along with Gothic tracery patterns, in the Catholic churches in Castroville, Lacoste (painted over), and Fredericksburg.

Champion Store and Restaurant, Port Isabel

AREA: Exterior facade
LOCATION: Walls
DECORATION: Freehand painting
SUBJECT: Fish murals

The front facade of the Champion Store and Restaurant (ca. early twentieth century) in Port Isabel near Brownsville displays the only known painting of ocean strata and one of the few examples of exterior decoration. Located in a popular South Texas fishing town, the brick building has two levels divided by architectural features with freehand painted marine life appropriately scaled and grouped in horizontal patterns. The painting shows sailfish, catfish, flounder, and shark as well as other marine creatures like squid, crabs, and turtles. Faded colors vary from blues and greens to browns, grays and cream.

McNay Residence (now McNay Art Museum, San Antonio). The foyer ceiling is decorated with stencilling dating from ca. 1920s–1930s. *(Courtesy University of Texas Institute of Texan Cultures, San Antonio.)*

FOUR

Contrasts: 1925 – 1950s

Fɴᴏᴍ 1925 ᴛᴏ ᴛʜᴇ 1950s, Texans exhibited a new spirit. The passing of the Great Depression and the turmoil of World War II brought an accelerated influx of war-related goods and services, as well as new construction and planned suburban communities in metropolitan areas such as Houston and Dallas. The result was a distinct clash between traditionalism and modernism — a clash that also helped to define the nature of interior decorative painting. While Texas builders and designers continued to adhere to the vernacular, they also adopted fashionable architectural styles: Spanish Colonial Revival, Italian Renaissance Revival, and Art Deco. The twenty-five-year period can be characterized by a blend of art and technology with an emphasis on high style. Buildings that contain decorative painting from the era are largely commercial structures like movie theaters or more mundane buildings like federal post offices.

In contrast, suburban homes reflected traditional images, homemade attitudes, and middle-class lifestyles. Despite the pretense of international concepts in Texas (and even some artistic influence from Hollywood films), the overriding message stressed the American vernacular and the American consumer.

To retain traditional values in their designs, American architects combined new technology with historical imagery. The result was a revival of architectural styles. Examples include Spanish Colonial Revival buildings inspired by the American Southwest as well as Italian Renaissance Revival structures influenced by Italian villas. Stimulated by national designers such as Paul Cret, Bernard Maybeck, Julia Morgan, Addison Mizner, and Georgia O'Keeffe, these styles articulated theories of informal ambience, regional interpretation, asymmetrical dominance, human scale, and environmental sitings. Developing as a truly American expression, suburbs blossomed in Palm Beach, Coral Gables, Austin, San Antonio, Beverly Hills, Santa Barbara, and

San Diego. White stucco walls, red-tile roofs, simplified classical arches, carved wooden doors, wood beamed ceilings, decorative tile trim, and wrought iron railings became the style of choice. Decorative painting usually appeared on frieze or ceiling areas, with motifs in geometric or classical designs rendered in stencilling or freehand painting.

Spanish Colonial Revival examples were particularly popular in Texas and date from 1920 to 1940; decorative painting was added within one to five years of construction. As picturesque examples of the southwestern character, they embody the symbolic personality of Texas through materials, motifs, shaping, and ambience. They are also a strong reflection of the rugged frontier spirit of a developing area. The Spanish Colonial Revival style gained wide acceptance in commercial buildings, but it was also used for residential and religious structures. Color blended subdued earth tones with cream white to create contrast in value. Similar in design, the less popular Italian Renaissance Revival style with its Mediterranean influences developed at the same time. It illustrated a more diverse palette in dull shades of many hues.

In San Antonio a number of distinctive houses date from the 1920s. In Austin an excellent collection of buildings on the University of Texas campus include stencil decoration that dates to the 1930s. Dallas buildings exhibit a wide variety of both styles, but the Highland Park Village Theater — in the Spanish Colonial Revival style — is particularly recognized for its panoramic murals. Varying from sophisticated to vernacular, these revival-style buildings generally follow national models, but are often grander in scale. Frequently offering an abundance of decoration, interiors feature embellished walls or ceilings with paintings often placed on or between wooden beams. Typical motifs include geometric patterns based on American Indian designs, murals derived from Texas or European history, western landscapes, and religious subjects.

Paralleling revival-style developments and displaying significant attributes of the modern movement, Art Deco prospered throughout the United States between the 1920s and the 1930s. As a stepchild of the French expression, Art Deco quickly took on a distinctly American character, blending traditionalism and modernism. Designs inspired by Futurism, Cubism, and the Bauhaus and influenced by the cultures of Egypt, Mexico, and Africa often emphasized historical themes as well as machine production. Proponents — who personalized the style — included Le Corbusier, Emile Jacques Ruhlmann, Syrie Maugham, Rene Lalique, Richard Neutra, and Donald Deskey. Designs emphasized geometry, synthetic materials, and function and were often inspired by period automobiles, ocean liners, and movies. Frequently expressing drama and fantasy, structures vary substantially in materials, balance, shaping, scale, and color. During the decade, characteristic stencilling and freehand painting in geometric patterns, figure forms, foliage interpretations, or urban landscapes were applied only on walls or ceilings. Colors varied from bright to delicate, with combinations of red, blue, and yellow mixed with white and black or muted shades of beige, white, gray, and pink.

Numerous surviving Art Deco structures with interior ornamentation date from the 1920s to the 1940s, with decorative painting often added within one year of construction, suggesting a planned interrelationship between construction and ornamentation. Examples include federal post offices, numerous commercial buildings and movie theaters from the 1940s.

High style, regional, and vernacular interpretations appear throughout the state, even though the style diminished in national popularity during the late 1930s. Paintings follow various national design models, but are often simplified and personalized into new contextual images. Two examples include federal post offices and regional movie theaters. Frequently embracing Art Deco features, their designs are modified by traditional or local interpretations. And within this context, decorative painting is either modern, regional, or a combination of both.

Government buildings often offer the best expressions of high style Art Deco. Two of the most noteworthy structures include the Hall of State (ca. 1935 – 1936) at Fair Park in Dallas and the city hall (ca. 1937 – 1939) in Houston. In both, exterior and interior planning articulates design harmony with continuity in scale, balance, and character. Rendered primarily on walls and ceilings, the decorative painting is freehand in an oil-base medium. Subjects and motifs vary significantly, with a distinct focus on Texas as depicted through its history, culture, and environment. The colors mirror this concept, maintaining a strong emphasis on earth tones rather than bright hues or muted shades.

Federal post offices offer good examples of simplified contextual images within regional settings. Generally identified by the terms PWA (Public Works Administration) or WPA (Works Progress Administration) architecture, their Art Deco designs promote linear features, monumental shapes, and light colored facades. To assure consistency in design, the federal government determined the overall architectural character. Interiors reflect exteriors, but often lack three dimensional architectural embellishment. Surface ornamentation consists primarily of decorative painting in the form of high quality murals commissioned by the Federal Arts Project (1935 – 1943) under the Section of Fine Arts. Juried on their intrinsic relationship to a lobby setting, and purchased with just one percent of the federal budget, murals were selected by knowledgeable experts from open, anonymous competitions held at national, regional, and state levels. They were intended to move people sentimentally, politically, and aesthetically, with themes focused on American history, the family, everyday American life, regional locales, transportation, and local industry. The portrayals are conservative, so the audience senses a dialogue with an old friend.

Located in large Texas cities and small Texas towns, extant post offices with lobby murals date from the 1930s and 1940s. Sixty-seven murals — executed at the time of construction — serve as constant reminders of the American way and the common man. In Texas, the most frequent themes are cowboys, cattle, farming, and pioneer heritage, concepts well illustrated in Amarillo, Ranger, Robstown, Seymour, Quanah, Gatesville, San Antonio, Anson, and Clifton. Many of the murals reflect popular art and evoke the flavor of American scene painting. Often the artists garnering commissions in Texas were native born or residents of the state, and they continued to gain popularity on a state, regional, and national basis after the Federal Arts program was completed.

While post offices illustrate the governmental image of American heritage, movie theaters represent the popular image of American taste and fantasy. They display designs blending high style, regional, and vernacular characteristics of various revival styles or of Art Deco. Defined by bold shapes and decorative colors, precursors usually included Egyptian temples, Italian gardens, Chinese palaces, Aztec buildings, French chateaus, ocean liner interiors, undersea environments, and the Wild West. The atmosphere enticed moviegoers with palatial scale, decorative enrichment, and theatrical drama. Interior walls often boasted landscapes, realistic figures, and large motifs, while ceilings depicted the sky, a tent, a building, or geometric patterns. Rendered primarily in stencilling and freehand painting, the decoration conveyed a palette featuring many hues specifically related to the historical theme.

Totaling over twenty in Texas, extant examples of movie theaters with interior ornamentation date from the late 1930s through the early 1950s, with decorative painting dating to the time of construction. The best examples exhibit the work of Eugene John Gilboe and are located in Dallas and Houston. The buildings vary in size, character, form, balance, materials, and coloration. While the exterior design primarily borrows from the national architectural model, the interior composition changes according to a particular theme. In Texas, it is common to see western landscapes, fantasy images, foliage motifs, and exotic environments. Colors usually reflect subjects and themes as well as fashionable national trends. There is much variety in hue, value, and intensity.

Other memorable examples of decorative painting from the period include unique murals executed by Italian prisoners of war in St. Mary's Catholic Church in Umbarger, the dairy scene in Parker Brothers Motor Company in Center, and the painting of valley life originally in the First National Bank (now in the post office) at Harlingen. This particular group illustrates the wide diversity of Texas decorative painting, the range of historical subjects, and the impact of popular culture.

Luchesse-Walker House, San Antonio

AREA: Living Room (alcove)
SIZE OF ALCOVE: 15′ – 8″ wide × 8′ – 6″
  deep × 10′ – 0″ high
LOCATION: Walls
DECORATION: Freehand painting
SUBJECT: Italian garden scene
ARTIST: Frank Cloonan
DATE: After ca. 1926

The Luchesse-Walker House (ca. 1926) in San Antonio contains a trompe l'oeil mural illustrating a formal Italian garden scene, an important subject for Latin cultures. Built for leading boot manufacturer Joe Luchesse and his wife, it epitomizes the popular Italian and Spanish Colonial Revival styles. Reflecting the owner's heritage, classical architectural features are repeated throughout the house and in the mural. Painted freehand on the living room wall, the mural extends the viewer's perception of space through the representation of a courtyard with arches, columns, and a balustrade. Garden colors emphasize shades of green, cream, pink, and brown. Cultural influences continue on the den frieze through Japanese landscape scenes, including Mount Fuji. Although expertly interwoven with the architectural features, the oriental selection is unusual. Both intricate, detailed artistic compositions are by skilled San Antonio artist Frank Cloonan. As recorded in the *City Directory of San Antonio* during the 1920s and the *Southern Messenger* for December 25, 1919, he specialized in paint supplies and church decorating under the title of "Cloonan and Osborn." The firm was located at 329 St. Mary's Street.

Landa House, San Antonio

AREA: Entrance Hall
SIZE: 21′ – 0″ wide × 21′ – 0″ long × 25′ – 0″ high
LOCATION: Ceiling (vaulted)
DECORATION: Stencilling, infill painting, freehand painting
ARTIST: Kindred McLeary
DATE: ca. 1928

The Landa House (ca. 1928), located in a fashionable San Antonio neighborhood, portrays romantic, classical illusions of European elegance. Built for wealthy German entrepreneur Harry Landa (December 20, 1861 – December 1951) and his wife Hannah, who had recently moved from nearby New Braunfels, it was designed in the popular Mediterranean style by Ernst B. Hayes and architect Robert Kelley. The spacious interior has two rooms with decorative painting. An impressive, two-story entrance hall displays sophisticated ornamentation on a vaulted plaster ceiling. Expressing sensitivity between the structure and the decoration, artist Kindred McLeary rendered high style motifs with great attention to the volume of space and the scale of decoration. The painting emphasizes classical designs such as cherubs, acanthus leaves, vases, medallions, and nudes — subjects often found in Italian villas. Appearing on top of an allover stencil pattern background, the motifs are well delineated in gold, blue-green, brown, and rust — a popular 1920s and 1930s palette.

Hidalgo County Bank and Trust Company, Mercedes

AREA: Lobby
LOCATION: Ceiling
DECORATION: Stencilling
ARTIST: F. Henzel and Company, San Antonio
DATE: ca. 1928

The Hidalgo County Bank and Trust Company (ca. 1927) in Mercedes is one of the few surviving south Texas structures with extant decoration. Formerly known as the Bank Building and Realty Company, it was designed by prominent San Antonio architect Ralph H. Cameron with construction costing $85,000. According to bank letters, Cameron recommended the San Antonio firm of F. Henzel and Company for the decorative painting. An authorized list of expenditures and contracts for the building found in old minute books indicates F. Henzel and Company proposed a fee of $1225 to paint the lobby ceiling. Applied to ten wood beams, the stencil patterns include striped bands, circular medallions, and acanthus leaf scrolls that imitate published national motifs and emphasize the then-popular concept of stylized decoration on prominent architectural features. Dull colors appear throughout in medium value shades of green, gold, and orange on a dark brown surface — again, a popular 1920s and 1930s palette.

Elks Lodge, Fort Worth

AREA: Lounge (first floor)
SIZE: Approximately 36' – 0" wide × 48' – 0"
   long × 10' – 6" high
LOCATION: Ceiling
DECORATION: Background stencil
DATE: ca. 1928
Photograph: Dan Hatzenbuehler

The Elks Lodge (ca. 1928) in Fort Worth — now owned by the YWCA — contains a fine example of background stencilling. Designed by the local architectural firm of Wyatt C. Hedrick, the modified Georgian structure originally had decoration in the lounge and auditorium. Conceived by interior decorator Dorothy Bacon of the local Ellison's Studio, the first floor lounge conveys an "antique Spanish" ambiance, while the auditorium (now painted over) illustrated a "purely Georgian" concept. Painting contractor D. C. Downs did not record the artist's name. Pseudo-historic in character, the lounge decoration imitates lace-like patterns confined within a ceiling area of nine rectangular bays. The overall painted surface is dull gold, creating the "positive" image of the pattern, while the applied stencil decoration is dull green, creating the "negative" background effect. In essence, the effect creates a reverse image. The overall design has a powerful scale with patterns similar to Spanish yeseria (or carved stone) decoration.

Gulf Building, Houston

AREA: Lobby
LOCATION: Walls
DECORATION: Freehand painting
ARTIST: Vincent Maragolitti
DATE: ca. 1929
PHOTOGRAPH: Old rendering from leasing
   brochure

The Gulf Building (ca. 1929) in Houston, built for company president Jesse H. Jones, and now a part of Texas Commerce Bank, contains one of three known examples of fresco painting. The Art Deco design represents the collaboration of prominent local architect Alfred C. Finn in association with New Yorkers Kenneth Franzenheim and J. E. R. Carpenter. The original leasing brochure describes eight lobby murals "illustrating the history of Texas, executed in wet fresco. The subjects are Aboriginal Indians, circa 1500; Landing of LaSalle, Matagorda Bay, 1685; Spanish Domination, 1770; Mexican Ascendancy, 1821; The Fall of the Alamo, 1836; Capture of Santa Anna, 1836; Houston, capital of the Republic of Texas, 1837, and Modern Houston. . . . The paint applied to wet plaster is absorbed into the plaster in such a manner that the color becomes an integral part of the material." Fresco painting is difficult, because surface area limitations play against the drying time of the plaster. The San Antonio post office murals, similar to these designs, and those in the Baytown post office, also exemplify a fresco technique. Executed by New Yorker Vincent Maragolitti, these freehand paintings show color variety, compositional preplanning, and large scale. Historical subjects were quite popular and were placed in commercial buildings where there was heavy traffic.

First Baptist Church, Amarillo

AREA: Vestibule
LOCATION: Walls and ceiling
DECORATION: Stencilling, infill painting
ARTIST: J. Charles Schnorr
DATE: ca. 1930

The First Baptist Church (ca. 1929 – 1930) in Amarillo is the only known Baptist church in Texas with decorative painting. Constructed at a cost of $500,000, this classically inspired structure is the collaborative work of St. Louis architect Gabriel Ferrand and Amarillo architect Guy A. Carlander (who had designed the previous parish church in 1908). The main church interior consists of a vestibule, an auditorium, and a sanctuary — all containing decoration integrated with the architectural features or applied to a flat surface and resembling work found in central Europe. Artist J. Charles Schnorr of New York and Pueblo, Colorado, ornamented the space. According to newspaper accounts, he was also commissioned to decorate the Pueblo County Courthouse in Colorado, the Capitol Hotel in Amarillo, the Church of the Immaculate Conception in Albuquerque, and the Hippodrome in New York.

His signature in this church is a distinct, preplanned interplay of structure and decoration using a "Tiffany style." The *Amarillo Sunday News Globe* of August 3, 1930, reported that the internationally famous artist was "descended from a long line of noted artists and noblemen, grandson of the Baron Jacob Carizovalt Von Schnorr of Germany. . . . Schnorr created the design used in the new church especially for protestant churches, and the local building is the first to be decorated in that design." Executed in about two months, the curved pattern illustrates an excellent outline stencil method with discernible brown dashed lines defining the motif shapes, typically rendered on plaster surfaces in water-base paint. Common period colors, some with shaded gradation, include blue-gray, turquoise, avocado green, gold, orange, and cream.

Village Theater, Dallas

AREA: Lobby
LOCATION: Walls
DECORATION: Freehand painting
SUBJECT: Early Americana and Texas history
ARTIST: James Buchanan Winn and Reveau
Bassett
DATE: ca. 1931

The Village Theater (ca. 1931) in the Highland Park suburb of Dallas is one of the most lavish, ornate movie houses in the state. Designed by Dallas architects Hugh Prather, Sr., and James Cheek, it represents the "rural Spanish village" from the 1929 Bar-celona International Exposition. Decorated just after construction, the interior is by local artists James Buchanan Winn and Reveau Bassett, who also worked on the State of Texas Building. Done in the popular Spanish theme, the foyer ceiling imitates geometric tile patterns while the lobby area displays a panoramic mural that portrays early American history. A landscape on the stairway walls includes Indians and explorers in a southwestern locale. The palette of green, brown, gold, rust and blue is typical. Because of its huge scale, it is probable the oil-on-canvas project was completed on location rather than in a studio. Overall, the decorative painting appropriately characterizes movie-theater art and popular culture in Texas during the 1930s.

Main Building and Student Union, The University of Texas at Austin

AREA: Main Building (formerly the Library), Hall of Texas Room
LOCATION: Ceiling
AREA: Student Union, Men's Lounge
LOCATION: Walls and ceiling
DECORATION: Stencilling, infill painting, freehand painting
ARTIST: Eugene John Gilboe
DATE: 1933
PHOTOGRAPH: Mary Helen Pratte (above), Buie Harwood (facing page)

The University of Texas at Austin has more extant decorative painting than any other Texas school. Designed by supervising university architect Robert Leon White in association with well-known Philadel-

phia architect Paul Philippe Cret, the inner mall buildings reflect the popular Spanish Colonial Revival and Beaux Arts styles. Located on the center campus axis, the Main Building (ca. 1933) is a monumental symbol of Texas heritage and academic grandeur. Formerly known as the "Library," it originally had twelve rooms embellished by experienced master decorator Eugene John Gilboe. Initially commissioned to decorate at least ten rooms in the Student Union, Gilboe subsequently submitted a proposal to decorate the Main Building for $12,000. Correspondence with W. J. Battle, chairman of the Building Committee, indicates the submission of a series of sketches, primarily watercolors illustrating the final design decisions made between the architect, the patrons, and the artist.

Meticulously preplanned, the paintings in the Hall of Texas (also known as the Business and Social Sciences Reading Room) illustrate Gilboe's integration of decoration with architectural features. In the northwest wing the artist painted various periods of Texas history, including Aztec culture, Indian Texas, Spanish conquest, French colonization, Spanish settlement, Mexican independence, American settlement, the Texas revolution, the Texas Republic, Texas statehood, Confederate Texas, and the first fifty years of the university. W. J. Battle wrote to colleagues that complementing this image, "on the brackets supporting the ends of the ceiling beams are painted the national arms of the chief stocks [nationalities] that make up the population of Texas. . . ."

Throughout the design, there are geometric shapes, curved patterns, color bands, and stylized motifs — all characteristic of Gilboe's early work. Many of these same features are equally well conceived in the Hall of Noble Words (also known as the Humanities Reading Room), which occupies the opposite building wing. In June 1933, W. J. Battle stated that he wanted subjects to symbolize the dependency of literature on the printing press and to inspire "utterances appropriate to the function of the room as an educational agency." Both spaces include stencil and freehand decoration on beams, ceilings, and friezes in a flat manner that enhances the stylized effect. Typical Spanish Colonial Revival colors complement this image: hues of red, gold, green, blue, white, and black on a dark brown background.

The renderings in the Student Union are signed "Eugene Gilboe, Decorator, Dallas." Following work at the university, Gilboe painted a mural in the Stoneleigh Apartment Hotel in Dallas where he lived, and later one in the Epperson Building in Houston. The latter was a lobby mural of a large Viking ship — as described in the *Houston Chronicle* for July 28, 1935 — "painted in a flat modernistic conventional design with no perspective."

Trained at the Oslo Art Academy as well as with recognized English and German masters, Norwegian Gilboe (September 23, 1881 – November 14, 1964) personified the European immigrant artist. After arriving in the United States in 1900, he worked for prominent New York studios including Baumgartens, Rambusches, and Wilmer A. French Company. He completed projects in Cincinnati, Minneapolis, Duluth, and Seattle before coming to Texas in 1932. Gilboe first settled in Dallas, then moved to Austin to work on several projects. The muralist brought over thirty years experience as an accomplished artist when the University of Texas contract was awarded.

In 1937, Gilboe was listed in the *Dallas City Directory* at Wycliff Avenue, and until 1940 he was in business at the Great National Life Building with

George A. Franklin as "Franklin and Gilboe" painters and decorators. Gilboe became well known during the 1940s for his decoration of movie theaters, examples of which are located in Dallas, Fort Worth, and Houston.

Chemistry Building, The University of Texas at Austin

AREA: Lecture Theater and Old Library
SIZE OF THEATER: Approximately 50′ – 0″
wide × 50′ – 0″ long × 25′ – 0″ high
SIZE OF LIBRARY: approximately 25′ – 0″
wide × 50′ – 0″ long × 18′ – 0″ high
LOCATION: Ceilings
DECORATION: Stencilling, infill painting, freehand painting
DATE: ca. 1929-1930s
PHOTOGRAPH: Mary Helen Pratte
RESTORATION: Buie Harwood and Betty McKee Treanor

Educational symbols are prominent features in the Old Chemistry Building, now called Welch Hall (ca. 1929), on the campus of the University of Texas at Austin. Designed by Dallas architect Herbert M. Greene, the building epitomizes the Spanish Colonial Revival style so typical throughout the campus. The old lecture theater and the old Mallet Library in Welch Hall contain elaborate decorative stencilling rendered in a southwestern Spanish flavor. The decorative ceilings in both areas incorporate colors sympathetic to the period, including gold, orange, red, and blue-green on a dark brown background. As noted in the 1929 construction documents, chemical symbols were incorporated in the lecture theater design, dramatizing the educational significance of the space. Those noted in the documents and their chemical reference include the sun (gold), Venus (copper), Mars (iron), antimony, Jupiter (tin), Saturn (lead), Mercury (mercury), and sulfur. Although the architect's original plans do not indicate specific designs for the rooms or the artist's name, it is possible that Eugene John Gilboe completed the decoration while he was working on other campus buildings. The decorative character is similar to his other work.

Austin Public Library, Austin

AREA: Loggia
SIZE: Approximately 12' – 3" wide × 29' – o"
 long × 18' – o" high
LOCATION: Ceiling (on groin vault)
DECORATION: Stencilling, infill painting, freehand
 painting
ARTISTS: Harold Jessen and Peter Allidi
DATE: ca. 1933
PHOTOGRAPH: Mary Helen Pratte

The old Austin Public Library (ca. 1933) has one of the few remaining examples of painted exterior decoration. Designed in the popular Italian Renaissance Revival style by architect H. F. Kuehne, the loggia ceiling design is in complete harmony with the structure. Decorator Peter Allidi (July 23, 1885 – September 27, 1948) and Austin architect Harold E. Jessen (October 27, 1908 – December 17, 1979) received the commission to decorate the ceiling in 1933. Allidi, born in Switzerland, listed his occupation as artist and interior decorator, having recently completed decoration in the architecture library of Goldsmith Hall on the University of Texas campus. Jessen was a student assistant on the project along with classmate James Hammond.

The ceiling designs, similar to those in Jessen's children's book *Hubert the Lion*, portray fantasies mixed with classical motifs — an unusual combination of visual languages. Appropriately positioned on center axis and related to the curved building form, they include winged horses, classical vases, medallions, and arabesques. Rendered in water-base paint with an emphasis on linear quality, the stencilled, infilled and freehand painted designs repeat from one vault to another. Colors are pale shades of gold, gray, blue, and rust on a cream plaster ground, hues which integrate well with the building style. As was common practice, Allidi and Jessen signed their work in an obscure place.

Post Office, Pampa

AREA: Lobby
SIZE: Approximately 26' – 0" wide × 65' – 0"
    long × 22' – 6" high
LOCATION: Ceiling
DECORATION: Stencilling
DATE: ca. 1934

The post office in Pampa (ca. 1934) has the only known stencil decoration among Texas post offices. The $160,000 structure (which is more decorative and less utilitarian than most) was conceived in Washington prior to the depression, but the expenditure was considered a necessity because the town was prospering and growing rapidly at the time. Designed by Dallas architects Dewitt and Washburn, assisted by T. P. Lippincott of Philadelphia, it evokes a modern Spanish Southwest character with cream colored walls and a red tile roof. The impressive lobby — which occupies fully one-third of the total floor space — is the highlight of the building. The *Pampa Daily News* described the ceiling on opening day, August 7, 1934, as "divided into five major divisions, and these are subdivided by false beams. There are 28 panels." Spanish, Navajo, Aztec, and Egyptian motifs cover all surfaces, with designs in green, gold, red, blue, and cream on a dark brown background. From six to ten workmen labored for two months on portable scaffolds and used $800 worth of twenty-three-carat gold leaf to create the effect.

State of Texas Building, Dallas

AREA: Hall of State
LOCATION: Walls
DECORATION: Stencilling (ceiling), freehand
    painting
MURAL SIZE: Each 80' – 0" wide × 30' – 0" high
TITLE: *Texas of History* and *Texas of Today*
ARTISTS: Eugene Savage assisted by James
    Buchanan Winn and Reveau Bassett
DATE: ca. 1935 – 1936
PHOTOGRAPH: Dallas Historical Society, Dallas

The State of Texas Building (ca. 1935 – 1936), located in the Texas Centennial Exposition site in Fair Park, contains a grand space decorated in a grand manner. As a part of the centennial complex designed by chief architect and Dallas native George Dahl, in association with prominent consultant Paul Cret of Philadelphia, the building highlights an impressive

collection of modern buildings with decorative painting. The Art Deco structure, positioned on a prominent landscaped axis, is by Houston architect Donald Barthelme who worked with ten other firms. While several rooms in the building are decorated, the Hall of State is the most elaborate design statement. Grand in scale, concept, and execution, it features murals by prominent artists of the time. Internationally known Eugene Savage spearheaded a team composed of artists James Buchanan Winn, Reveau Bassett, and George Davidson.

Having studied previously in Rome, Indiana-born Savage joined the faculty at Yale University in 1925 before becoming "Commissioner of Painting of the Fine Arts Commission of the United States" (a position corresponding to a cabinet post). Texas native Winn studied in St. Louis and at the Académie Juliane in Paris, developing expertise in large-scale murals and figure painting. Dallas native Bassett apprenticed with various artists before starting a teaching career at the Dallas Art Institute, where he further developed abilities in wildlife painting. Polish-born Davidson also studied with various artists, worked with Savage at Yale, and won the 1926 gold medal for mural painting from the New York Architectural League.

Reports of the time indicate the project took just five months to complete and cost $30,000. Claims were made suggesting the murals were the largest executed in oil since Tintoretto's Venetian masterpiece *Paradise* at the Doges Palace.

As stated by artist Savage in the centennial celebration brochure of 1936, the north wall emphasizes the years in Texas' history from "the advent of the first white man to the founding of the Republic." Featured subjects include explorers, Indians, Northern armies, the Battle of Conception, the Battle of the Alamo, the Texas Republic, and over five historic portraits. Representing statehood, the south wall features the period following days of the Republic, natural resource development, cultural progress, and commercial development. Historical characters are labelled where scale and complexity of the subject permit. Colors vary throughout the composition, and harmonize well with the stencilled ceiling treatment by Davidson. Using southwestern images, the ceiling incorporates Aztec motifs, a West Texas road runner, an armadillo, and an abstraction of land and sea in green, brown, blue, and gold. The overall effect captivates as well as educates the viewer.

City Hall, Houston

AREA: Lobby

SIZE: Approximately 25′ – 0″ wide × 25′ – 0″
  long × 20′ – 0″ high

LOCATION: Ceiling

DECORATION: Stencilling, infill painting, freehand
  painting

TITLE: North wall — *O Great City of*
  Vision — Beautiful — Strong

East wall — *A Goddess in purpose and mind . . .*
  We fight

South wall — *For the cause of honor — Virtue*

West wall — *Liberty pledged to the glory of*
  mighty Houston

ARTISTS: Daniel MacMorris, assisted by Grace
  Spaulding John and Ruth Pershing Uhler

DATE: ca. 1939

PHOTOGRAPH: *Houston Chronicle*, Sunday
  November 5, 1939 (courtesy Public Library,
  Texas Collection, Houston)

The Houston city hall (ca. 1937 – 1939) is the best
example of modern Art Deco decoration totally integrated with a building's architectural style. Designed
by prominent Houston architect Joseph Finger, of
Austrian descent, the building cost over a million
dollars with a mural commission of $6000. Extant
decoration includes lobby murals by noted Kansas
City artist Daniel MacMorris assisted by Houston artists Grace Spaulding John and Ruth Pershing Uhler.
John met MacMorris while both pursued Tiffany
Foundation fellowships. They later made contact
with Uhler, who was in charge of the Department of
Design at the Museum of Fine Arts. Most of the work
for the Houston building was executed at the Nelson
Memorial Galleries in Kansas City, where MacMorris developed initial design sketches in half-inch scale.
Later he prepared larger drawings of individual panels. Finally, he worked on canvas attached to a large
wall surface, completing the project in five months.

The four murals contain individual vignettes of figures (some classically draped), animals, and trees
symbolically representing Houston's culture, industry, law, and government. Each is titled to convey the
appropriate message. A perimeter border of flowers,
animal heads, palm fronds, and cactus frame and
unify the composition. Subdued, monochromatic

oil-base paints in rose, pink, blue-green, brown, and white harmonize with the stylistic character of the building and with specific architectural features. Overall, this is a high style illustration of decorative painting, followed later in Texas by more regional interpretations.

Baytown

San Antonio

Post Offices in Baytown, Amarillo, Ranger, Robstown, Seymour, Quanah, Gatesville, San Antonio

MURALS: Federal Arts Project
AREA: Lobby
LOCATION: Wall
DECORATION: Freehand painting

Baytown (Goose Creek)
PHOTOGRAPH: ca. 1938, Postmaster's Collection, Baytown

This illustration shows the typical building style used for Texas post offices during the 1930s and 1940s.

Amarillo (now the J. Marvin Jones Federal Building and U.S. Courthouse)
MURAL SIZE: 18' – 0" wide × 5' – 0" high
TITLE: *Cattle Loading*
ARTIST: Julius Woeltz
DATE: ca. 1940

Representing typical Panhandle culture, this extensive composition includes five murals of western ranch life. The two Amarillo men sitting on the fence are a Mr. Morgan (white shirt) and a Mr. Burgess (yellow jacket).

Ranger
Mural Size: 11' – 0" wide × 4' – 8" high
TITLE: *Crossroads Town*
ARTIST: Emil Bisttram
DATE: ca. 1939

This mural portrays a small Texas town during the early 1900s and illustrates our pioneer heritage through typical western buildings and cowboys. The scene is reminiscent of American history as well as popular culture depicted in film.

Robstown
MURAL SIZE: 14' – 0" wide × 4' – 6" high
TITLE: *Founding and Subsequent Development of Robstown, Texas*
ARTIST: Alice Reynolds
DATE: ca. 1941

Similar in character to *Saturday Evening Post* magazine covers, the mural portrays Robstown's transformation from a lonely railroad junction to a farming empire. The lady in the red dress is Mrs. Ella M. Beyettee, who came on the first excursion train and helped the artist gather research photographs.

Robstown

Amarillo

Gatesville

Seymour

    MURAL SIZE: 13' – 6" wide × 4' – 10" high
    TITLE: *Comanches*
    ARTIST: Tom Lea
    DATE: ca. 1942

Evoking images of life in the early West, Tom Lea's painting is a dramatic rendition of Comanche Indians. One of three by the well-known West Texas artist commissioned by the federal government, it captures his enduring attraction to action-oriented scenes with horses.

Quanah

    MURAL SIZE: 13' – 9" wide × 4' – 6" high
    TITLE: *Naming of Quanah*
    ARTIST: Jerry Bywaters
    DATE: ca. 1938

Comanche chief Quanah Parker is portrayed after the opening of the Panhandle area to white settlers and following his 1874 defeat at Palo Duro Canyon. The flat North Texas landscape includes the railroad, cowboys, and the nearby Medicine Mounds. The colors on this western landscape are limited shades of brown, gray, white and dull red.

Emulating the work of popular regionalist Thomas Hart Benton, prominent Dallas artist Jerry Bywaters (born May 21, 1906) conveys a rich contextual image — one appropriate to Texas as well as Federal Arts Projects. Bywaters produced four Texas post office murals in the 1940s while serving as a Southern Methodist University faculty member. Highly regarded in his profession, the artist had been associated with the Dallas Art Institute and the *Dallas News*. Later he served as director of the Dallas Museum of Fine Arts.

Gatesville

    MURAL SIZE: 10' – 0" wide × 5' – 2" high
    TITLE: *Off to Northern Markets*
    ARTIST: Joe DeYong
    DATE: ca. 1939

Joe DeYong, a California movie studio artist, went to some effort to illustrate a realistic Texas cattle drive. When notified in 1938 of his $630 commission, DeYong (who died in 1974) wrote the Gatesville postmaster requesting information about the structure, the name of a local photographer, and a sampling of Gatesville postcards. While this type of communication was typical during the period, it rarely survives to clarify artistic subjects. After completing the painting, the artist wrote that he wanted to show the head of the herd, or "point," a wrangler with saddle horses, and a cook with the chuck wagon. He also went on to say that the horses were usually branded on the left side as a courtesy to riders passing

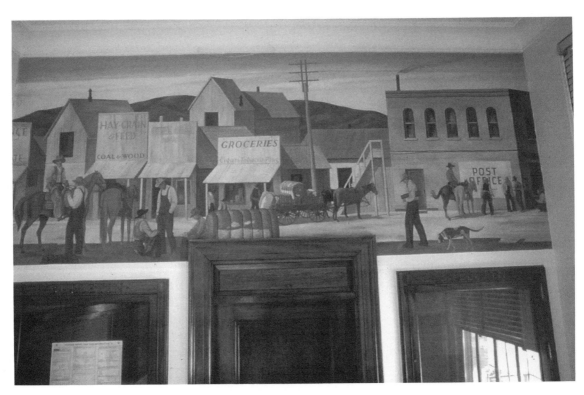

Ranger

on the right. Although he never journeyed to Texas before or during the 1939 installation, DeYong was knowledgeable of cowboy traditions because of an early Oklahoma association with movie stars Will Rogers and Tom Mix and through studies with noted artist Charles Russell.

San Antonio
    AREA: South Lobby
    LOCATION: Walls (frieze)
    DECORATION: Freehand painting (fresco)
    MURAL SIZE: 16 separate panels varying in size
    TITLE: *San Antonio's Importance in Texas History*
    ARTIST: Howard Cook
    DATE: ca. 1937
    PHOTOGRAPH: The University of Texas Institute of Texan Cultures, San Antonio and the Martha Freeman Collection.

San Antonio's "Downtown Station" (ca. 1937) contains one of two fresco murals in Texas. The one in San Antonio is by artist Howard Cook of Taos, New Mexico. Spanning 750 square feet with sixteen separate panels, the painting is the largest of all those commissioned for Texas post offices. Cook, well known and widely exhibited, was paid $12,000 for the project, which took twelve months to complete.

The post office itself was designed in the popular Classical Revival style by Texas architect Ralph H. Cameron with an exterior noticeably different in design and scale from other government Art Deco projects. Also distinguished by scale, the upper walls of the south lobby boast Cook's huge fresco, *San Antonio's Importance in Texas History*.

Cook drew preliminary cartoons for the work in his Taos studio and also experimented there with the technical aspects of fresco application and color mixing. Describing the project in the January 1942 edition of the *Magazine of Art*, he indicated a desire "to express in terms of color as well as design the excitement and sturdiness of exploration and pioneering, the drama and tragedy in the struggle for political freedom, the final opening of a full, settled life provided by the industry of man and fed by the wealth of natural resources." Consequently, the panels portray Spanish conquerors, colonial settlement, the Texas revolution, the Texas Republic, and Texas growth. It depicts all ethnic races in the state. Only one local man, shown as a padre on the south wall, was used as a model. As was typical of the period, the artist signed his work on a south panel depicting cowboys and cattle.

Quanah

St. Mary's Catholic Church, Umbarger

AREA: Apse
LOCATION: Wall
DECORATION: Freehand painting, stencilling (dado)
TITLE: *The Visitation*
ARTISTS: World War II era Italian POWs
DATE: ca. 1945
PHOTOGRAPH: Texas Historical Commission, Austin by Carol Kennedy and Linda Flory

St. Mary's Catholic Church (ca. 1930) in the rural farming community of Umbarger has the only known remaining examples of mural decoration by Italian prisoners of war. Reflecting previous social and economic conditions, this Panhandle structure is rather stark and plain outside, but it is richly decorated inside. There are elaborately detailed religious murals on the apse walls and stencilling applied throughout to embellish architectural features. The murals depict the Visitation and the Annunciation and are executed in an early Italian Renaissance style with a unique twist — the landscape shows the high flat plains surrounding Umbarger, with figures modelled after local school girls who posed for the artists. Drawing on their Italian and Catholic heritage, the untrained Italian artists came from a nearby internment camp. Their names are recorded as Archille Cattanei, Leonida Gorlato, Marid de Cristoford, Antonio Monetti, Enrico Zorzi, Dino Gambetti, Franco de Bello, Amedeo Maretto, and Carlo Sanvito. German parishioners commissioned the decoration.

Parker Brothers Motor Company, Center

AREA: Showroom
LOCATION: Wall
DECORATION: Freehand painting
SUBJECT: Dairy scene
ARTIST: A. Lafayette
DATE: ca. 1946

Parker Brothers Motor Company (ca. 1945) in the East Texas community of Center has the distinction of being the only known car dealership with a 1940s dairy scene painted on the wall. While the exterior is rather plain, the interior is definitely enlivened by the mural. Its subject — a woman, two men, and a cow — copies 1940s advertisements appearing in magazines, dairy journals, and billboards. It is also reminiscent of the work of popular *Saturday Evening Post* artist Norman Rockwell. Realistically rendered in a vignette format, the depiction is signed "A. Lafayette, ⅍ Billboard, Cincinnati, O." According to the owner who commissioned the project, Lafayette worked with the assistance of his seven-year-old grandson, spent two days in 1946 executing the paint-

ing, and was paid $25 for his efforts. Apparently the artist was en route to another town and needed money, so he asked to do the painting. His technique incorporates an infill method using perforated sheets placed against the wall to define forms and shapes. Colors are limited to traditional shades of brown, gold, gray, and white with an emphasis on gradation of value.

Broadway Theater, Galveston

AREA: Auditorium
LOCATION: Walls and ceiling
DECORATION: Freehand painting
ARTIST: Eugene John Gilboe
DATE: ca. 1947
PHOTOGRAPH: Martin Woods Collection, Dallas

The Broadway Theater (ca. 1947; now painted over) in Galveston is one of twenty-six Texas theaters decorated by artist Eugene John Gilboe between 1937 and 1952. Billed as a "suburban theater," it was an arena for spectacular escape providing live shows and feature films. Popular national decorative themes and Gilboe's own trademark motifs included an "atmospheric space," nautical subjects, southwestern Indian designs, regional history, and an exotic landscape. This theater emphasized the latter and had extensive murals featuring banana trees and palm leaves on the auditorium walls. The decorated ceiling combined some of the same concepts, but the composition was more stylized and geometric. Grand in

scale and elaborate in appearance, the design showed meticulous planning and close attention to detail — also characteristic of Gilboe's work, which reflected images popular in the 1940s.

The artist crisscrossed the state during the 1940s for either the Interstate Amusement Company or the Publix Theater Corporation, repeating the foliage motifs in other movie theaters. Comparable treatments are recorded in the Garden Oaks Theater (ca. 1947) in Houston, the Santa Rosa Theater (ca. 1947) in Houston, the Campus Theater (ca. 1949) in Denton, the Arlington Theater in Arlington, the Circle Theater (ca. 1947) in Dallas, and the Forest Theater (ca. 1949) in Dallas. Varying somewhat from the theme, he incorporated "amazing marine murals" showing fish through a ship's porthole and plants underwater on the walls in the Inwood Theater (ca. 1947) in Dallas. Similar in concept, highlights of a redecorated Majestic Theater (ca. 1921) were reported in the *Dallas Morning News* in October 1948. The "main (auditorium) ceiling," according to the paper, "is painted to create a feeling of moonlight, trellis work of a soft cactus green giving the effect of a flower

garden. . . . A huge floral mural covers the entire length of a twenty foot wall in the ladies lounge, painted in colors of charcoal purple, avocado green, mustard, and parchment." The colors, typical of Gilboe's palette, appear in other structures, along with terra cotta, coral, turquoise, blue, and brown. Gilboe's price for these projects depended on size. He charged anywhere from $2000 to $6000 — reasonable estimates for this type of work at this time.

Above. Gluck-Kadernoschka Place, Cat Spring (ca. 1860s; decoration ca. 1860s–1880s). BEDROOM: This detail of a European landscape scene includes a man in a costume dating from the 1830s to the 1860s and verifies the date of the decoration.

Left. McGregor-Grimm House, Winedale (ca. 1861; decoration ca. 1861–1868). PARLOR: A detail of the ceiling that includes a vase of fruit. The decoration was probably painted by Rudolph Melchior.

St. Paul's Lutheran Church, Serbin (ca. 1867–1871; decoration ca. 1871). NAVE: The church interior has feathered marbling on ten wooden columns with decoration by artist August Weber. COLUMN: This detail of feathered marbling is rendered in dark gray-green on a blue-gray background.

House of the Seasons, Jefferson (ca. 1872; decoration after ca. 1872). DOME: The ceiling detail includes trompe l'oeil panels and individualized classical figures representing the seasons. It was rendered on wooden boards by an unknown artist. *(Courtesy John Klein)*

Sterrett House, Beckville (ca. 1889, now destroyed; decoration after ca. 1889). PARLOR: This wall detail has a trompe l'oeil picture frame showing the Civil War battle between the *Monitor* and the *Merrimac* and graining on the door and stencilling on the frieze—vernacular decoration by an itinerant painter.

Marburger-Witte House, Shelby (ca. 1870s; decoration before ca. 1900).
PARLOR: A detail of the ceiling that shows the precise painting technique.

Addison-Gandy House, Montgomery (ca. 1892; decoration after ca. 1892).
BEDROOM: One door in this room has a unique grained portrait of a well defined bearded face, possibly that of the artist or owner.

St. Mary's Catholic Church, Praha (ca. 1895; decoration ca. 1895). NAVE AND APSE: The ceiling and upper walls are embellished with trompe l'oeil European images commissioned by Czech immigrants and executed on wooden boards by artist Gottfried Flury.

Eichholt-Guderian-Kruse House, Brenham area (ca. 1865, 1929; decoration ca. 1902). PARLOR: A rare checkerboard floor with alternating stars was painted by artist Charles Meister in rust, gray and blue. BEDROOM: This ceiling medallion shows a woman's portrait with a heart-shaped pin enclosing the letters "AB," possibly referring to Meister's daughter Hattie Anna Bertha.

Warren-Crowell House, Terrell (ca. 1903–1904; decoration ca. 1904). DINING ROOM: The Art Nouveau wall decoration with floral patterns, rendered through infill and freehand painting, is a unique design by Keith and Company of Kansas City. *(Courtesy Dan Hatzenbuehler)*

Dieringer-Kuester-McChesney House, Lindenau (ca. 1910; decoration ca. 1910). ENTRY HALL: The rare all-over stencilling, resembling wallpaper, above a marbled dado illustrates the work of local Texas artist Gustav Luerssen (a Swedish immigrant) for a German farm family. *(Courtesy Mary Helen Pratte)*

Burton-Merritt House, McKinney (ca. 1905; decoration ca. 1912–1915). ENTRY: The canvas ceiling mural, which imitates eighteenth-century French Rococo designs, depicts a partially draped female surrounded by cupids in a romantic landscape. The mural is in one of five rooms decorated with sophisticated images by artist Peter Plotkin. (*Courtesy Dan Hatzenbuehler.*)

St. Mary's Catholic Church, High Hill (ca. 1905–1906; decoration ca. 1912). NAVE AND SANCTUARY: The decorative painting on the ceiling and columns imitate central European designs similar to those along the Rhine River, with patterns derived from books in the library of San Antonio artist Ferdinand Stockert, who worked with fellow German Herman Kern on the project.

Kruppa-Zimmerhanzel House, Cistern (ca. 1910; decoration ca. 1912–1915). PARLOR: The Art Nouveau stencil decoration on the walls came from patterns published in the "Sereco Paint Catalog" of 1911 by Sears, Roebuck and Company. A Czech painter complemented the design with a freehand rendition of clouds and flower bouquets on the ceiling. *(Courtesy Mary Helen Pratte.)*

Ascension Church, Moravia (ca. 1912–1913; decoration ca. 1923). APSE: The walls, painted by Donecker and Sons, are extensively covered with trompe l'oeil decorations.

Champion Store and Restaurant, Port Isabel (ca. early 20th century). EXTERIOR FACADE: The front of this brick building displays painted illustrations of marine creatures. It is one of the few examples of exterior decoration.

Luchesse-Walker House, San Antonio (ca. 1926; decoration ca. 1926). LIVING ROOM: The trompe l'oeil Italian garden scene is by San Antonio artist Frank Cloonan.

Landa House, San Antonio (ca. 1928; decoration ca. 1928). ENTRANCE HALL: This two-story vaulted ceiling with elegant classical designs often found in Italian villas is in a Mediterranean style building and is the work of local artist Kindred McLeary.

LET ALL THE EARTH KEEP
SILENCE BEFORE HIM HAB 2. 20

First Baptist Church, Amarillo (ca. 1929–1930; decoration ca. 1930). VESTIBULE: This is the only known Baptist church in Texas with painted decoration. It was executed by the internationally famous German artist J. Charles Schnorr in a "Tiffany" style that incorporates an outline stencil method.

Chemistry Building, The University of Texas at Austin (ca. 1929; decoration after ca. 1929). LECTURE THEATER: Chemical symbols, dramatizing the educational significance of the space, are rendered on this ceiling in sympathetic period colors with a southwestern Spanish flavor. *(Courtesy Mary Helen Pratte)*

Main Building, The University of Texas at Austin (ca. 1933; decoration ca. 1933). LIBRARY-HALL OF TEXAS ROOM: Located in a Spanish Colonial Revival building, this ceiling portrays a monumental symbol of Texas heritage and academic grandeur and represents one of several projects by talented master decorator and Norwegian immigrant Eugene John Gilboe. *(Courtesy Mary Helen Pratte)*

CAUSE OF HONOR

City Hall, Houston (ca. 1937–1939; decoration ca. 1939). LOBBY: This ceiling detail is from one of several Art Deco murals representing Houston's culture, industry, law, and government, and was executed by noted Kansas City artist Daniel MacMorris, assisted by Houston artists Grace Spaulding John and Ruth Pershing Uhler. *(Courtesy Mary Helen Pratte.)*

Austin Public Library, Austin (ca. 1933; decoration ca. 1933). LOGGIA: This groin vaulted ceiling is one of the few remaining examples of exterior decoration. It was rendered in fantasy images mixed with classical motifs by artists Peter Allidi and Harold E. Jessen. *(Courtesy Mary Helen Pratte.)*

Post Office, Pampa (ca. 1934; decoration ca. 1934). LOBBY: The only known illustration of stencil decoration in Texas post offices, this ceiling is embellished with Spanish, Navajo, Aztec, and Egyptian motifs. Detail of stencil patterns shows the twenty-three-carat gold leaf used to create the decorative effect.

Post Office, Seymour (ca. 1940s; decoration ca. 1942). LOBBY: Evoking images of life in the early West, this mural—one of sixty-seven in the state—provides a dramatic rendition of Comanche Indians by well-known Texas artist Tom Lea.

Post Office, San Antonio (ca. 1937; decoration ca. 1937). SOUTH LOBBY: The fresco, *San Antonio's Importance in Texas History,* represents one of the largest commissions awarded for a Texas post office. The San Antonio post office interior features sixteen fresco murals by Taos artist Howard Cook.

Ridglea Theater, Fort Worth

AREA: Lobby
LOCATION: Walls
DECORATION: Freehand painting
SUBJECT: Pirates
DATE: ca. 1950
PHOTOGRAPH: Martin Woods Collection, Dallas

The Ridglea Theater (ca. 1950) in Fort Worth represents another example of Gilboe's work. Equally as large in scale as those in the Broadway Theater in Galveston, these lobby murals depict fantasies from popular literature — pirates in a boat surrounded by a palm tree landscape. Realistic in interpretation, the murals illustrate another of Gilboe's artistic accomplishments. Figures are the primary focus — frequently intertwined with a picturesque environment — and became a popular theme for his

projects. Similar concepts appeared in the 25th Street Theater in Waco, with chariot riders, and in the Esquire Theater (ca. 1948) in Amarillo, with cowboys on horseback in a stylized southwestern landscape, as well as in the earlier Esperson Building (ca. 1928) in Houston, which includes a biblical figure standing by an ancient well. Often the perspective is flat with images overlapping to show depth. Although a variety of paints were available to him, Gilboe worked primarily in an oil-base medium.

After a long and successful career as a muralist in New York and Texas, Gilboe retired to Dallas in 1953 with his third wife. While his projects may never be fully documented, those recorded to date number thirty-five completed in Texas between 1932 and 1952. They include institutional buildings, commercial structures, and movie theaters. Each offers a definitive, personalized view of Gilboe the "interior decorator."

First National Bank, Harlingen

AREA: Lobby
DECORATION: Freehand painting
MURAL SIZE: 38' – 0" wide × 11' – 0" high
TITLE: *Valley Industries*
ARTIST: Normah Knight
DATE: ca. 1951
PHOTOGRAPH: Normah Knight Collection,
    Harlingen

The First National Bank Building (ca. 1951), located in Harlingen and designed by architects Cocke,
Bowman, and York, formerly contained the large
mural *Valley Industries*. Relocated when the bank
expanded many years later, the mural now hangs in
the local post office and is one of the few surviving
examples of decorative painting in the area. Originally commissioned for a modernistic building, its
grand scale dominated the lobby. The composition,
divided into three paneled sections, portrays particular businesses associated with South Texas. As described in the *Valley Morning Star* of March 25,
1951, the center panel "represents the creation of the
Rio Grande Valley with Demeter, the Goddess of
Fertility, sowing her seeds to make the land
productive. . . . The left panel continues the tribute
to the Valley's agriculture. It shows water being
brought in for irrigation to provide a year round growing season. . . . The right hand panel is dominated by
the big figure of Zeus, the God of Electricity, hurling
lightning bolts. It represents the power brought in to
turn the wheels of machinery and enable the indus-
trialization of the Lower Rio Grande Valley."

Well-known local artist Normah Knight (born July
25, 1910) completed the triptych after careful research and an investigation of the surrounding ter-
rain. Born in Dallas, she studied at the Dallas Art
Institute, Southern Methodist University, the Juliane
Académie in Paris, and with noted artists in the
United States before settling in the Valley in 1931.
Having exhibited widely, she is listed in several editions of distinguished art biographies.

St. Cyril and Methodius Catholic Church, Shiner

AREA: Apse
LOCATION: Walls and ceiling
DECORATION: Freehand painting
SUBJECT: Christ in the Garden of Gethsemane
ARTIST: Edmond Fatjo
DATE: ca. 1954

St. Cyril and Methodius Catholic Church (ca. 1919) in the small German and Czech farm community of Shiner is unusual because the decoration was applied thirty-five years after initial construction. It has the only example of a panoramic religious mural on a domed ceiling. Designed in the Romanesque Revival style, the building is the work of noted San Antonio architect James Wahrenberger and builder Vincent Falbo. Construction cost $80,000.

Initially plain, the interiors were elaborately decorated in 1954 after repair and renovation was finished. Edmond Fatjo, trained at the Royal Art Academy in Berlin, is believed to have been the artist. He painted church interiors from 1925 to 1964, but there is little record of his activity in Texas. His artistic skill, however, is evident in this interior. Throughout the space, stencilled religious symbols accent arches, cornices, and frieze areas. But the most impressive design statement is the huge panoramic mural located on the apse ceiling — it realistically depicts Christ in the Garden of Gethsemane. Dark in value with an emphasis on blue and gray, the mural contrasts significantly with the lighter character of the interior, thereby contributing to a sense of religious awe. Artist Fatjo also embellished the choir area with a mural of St. Cecelia, patron saint of music.

APPENDICES

Glossary

Anthemion — A stylized honeysuckle motif used in Greek decoration.

Architrave — The bottom portion of an entablature in classical ordering; it often includes flat molding.

Brushes — Popular brushes for decorative painting include a fitch, a tapered sable brush for freehand painting; a stenciller, a round brush with short bristles; a mottler, a wide flat brush; a pencil, a narrow thin brush used for making lines; a blender, a small round brush for blending paint; and a stippler, a long flat brush used to create a textured surface. Brush numbers designate size, a larger number indicating a larger size.

Color — Color is an element of design defined by hue (color name), value (light or dark), and intensity or chroma (saturation or purity). The primary colors for paint pigment are red, blue, and yellow. Color quality and interpretation are affected by either natural or artificial light.

Column — The column is the central portion of a wall which includes a capital, shaft, and column base in classical ordering. Located between the frieze and the dado, it often contains pilasters which define the architectural composition.

Cornice — The top portion of an entablature in classical ordering with three-dimensional moldings.

Cracking — Cracking indicates a fractured looking surface caused from paint breaking into tiny sections. It results from an improper paint mixture, the wrong undercoat, or inadequate drying time.

Dado — Similar to a pedestal in classical ordering, a dado is approximately the lower three feet of a wall. It may be panelled or ornamented and is often capped by a chair rail.

Diaper — A diaper is an allover pattern, consisting of one or more small repetitive units of design.

Distemper Painting — Distemper painting mixes water with paint colors, glue, and whiting. Generally the effect is whiter or more tinted than using a mixture of only pure colors.

Forms — Forms are three-dimensional and have length, width, height, and depth. They may be organic or geometric in design such as a sphere, cube, or pyramid. In interior spaces, they include moldings, furniture, and decorative objects.

Freehand Painting — Freehand painting incorporates individual designs, usually pictorial images. Subjects are often isolated vignettes or extensive surface paintings such as landscape scenes, prominent buildings, nature motifs, classical and religious figures, or historical subjects.

Fresco Painting — Fresco painting is executed on wet plaster walls. The colors are made from an earth or mineral base ground into pure water. Depending on the amount of surface an artist can paint in one day, only a limited amount of wall or ceiling surface is "worked up." Historical references identify fresco painting as a type of distemper painting.

Frieze — The frieze is the upper portion of a wall in

classical ordering or the central decorated area of an entablature. The entablature includes a cornice, frieze, and architrave.

Graining — Graining imitates real wood, using at least three layers of different hues to create a trompe l'oeil (fool the eye) effect. Typically, graining is applied to interior architectural moldings and mantels. Tools include graining combs, rollers, and transfer plates. Colors vary according to the wood copied. Published nineteenth-century references often include instructional information as well as colored graining examples.

Guilloche — A band or border motif used in Greek decoration and characterized by overlapping or interlacing circular forms.

Infill Painting — Infill painting is similar to stencilling, and is also known as outline stencilling or pounce painting. It is identified by an enlarged scale, telltale guidelines, and the transfer method.

Kalsomine — Kalsomine is a mixture of size and pigment coating walls and ceilings. It was frequently made of zinc white mixed with glue and water, then heated to a jellied state.

Line — Line is an element of design used to define shapes and forms. It may be straight or curved, either vertical, horizontal, or diagonal, and has length but no breadth.

Marbling — Marbling uses highly skilled painting techniques to achieve a trompe l'oeil effect. Generally it is applied to baseboards, columns, or mantels. Application is all done by hand following specific published guidelines. Twentieth century publications refer to this decoration as marbleizing.

Oil Painting — Oil painting uses an oil-base substance for the mixture of paint colors. Application characteristics include opaque colors, long drying time, and strong color rendition.

Painting — Painting is the art of representing objects to the eye on a flat surface by means of line, shade, and color to convey artistic ideas. It also includes the paint application for the purpose of beautifying or preserving a surface. Specific terms describe different methods such as decorative painting, carriage painting, and easel painting. Other terms describe paint application such as watercolor, oil, and fresco.

Rinceau — A scroll and leaf motif, usually symmetrical and repetitive, used in Greek decoration

Shapes — Shapes are two-dimensional planes with length and width, but no depth. They are usually organic or geometric in design such as a circle, square or triangle. In interior spaces, they are the ceiling, walls, and floor which define the architectural envelope.

Spandrel — The panel or wall space between two adjoining arches and the horizontal line above them; most often seen in the separation between the apse and the nave in a church.

Stencilling — Stencilling is a mechanical, decorative process characterized by repeated pattern with colors conveyed in a flat, unshaded manner. Each pattern may be divided into various parts, requiring a different stencil plate for each separate color. The color cut away in the stencil plate constitutes a part of the pattern. The most common forms of stencilling are the block or solid stencil and the outline stencil.

Style — As used herein, the term style refers to a characteristic or specific design expression represented in art work or a particular historical period. It is usually long lasting in contrast to a short-lived fashion.

Watercolor — Watercolor painting uses a water base for the mixture of paint colors. Application characteristics include transparent colors, quick drying time, and soft effects.

Yeseria — Small polychromed lace-like patterns of plaster or stone relief used on the walls of Moorish-style rooms in Spanish buildings.

Inventory: Artists

*(Compiled by name, place or places of work,
working date or dates)*

Aceves, José: Borger, Mart, 1939
Allidi, Peter: Austin, 1930s
Ankrom, Francis: Canyon, 1938
Arnautoff, Victor: College Station, Linden,
    1930s
Arnest, Bernard: Wellington, 1939
Arpa, Jose: San Antonio, 1926
Babcock, Gertrude: College Station, 1940
Baker, W.: Fort Worth, 1930s
Ballard, _____: Palacios, 1900s
Bassett, Reveau: Dallas, 1930s
Beck, _____: Vernon, 1925
Beck, Theodore: Witchita Falls, 1919
Benecker, Anton: Schulenberg, 1896
Bisttram, Emil: Ranger, 1939
Boerder, F. J.: Dallas, 1936
Brage, B. H.: San Antonio, 1928
Brown, Frederick: Houston, 1936
Brunet, Adele: Dallas, 1930s
Bugbee, Harold: Dallas, Canyon, 1930s
Bywaters, Jerry: Dallas, Farmersville, Houston,
    Odessa, Paris, Trinity, 1930s – 1940s
Campbell, Charles: Kenedy, 1939
Carlew, Jacques: Dallas, 1920s?
Carnohan, Harry: Dallas, 1930s
Chavez, Edward: Center, 1941
Cherry, E. R.: Houston, 1890s – 1930s?
Cisneros, Antonio: Brownsville, 1940s
Cloonan, Frank: San Antonio, 1920s
Cook, Howard: San Antonio, Corpus Christi,
    1937 – 1941
Davidson, George: Dallas, 1936
Del Piño, José Moya: Alpine, 1940
DeYong, Joe: Gatesville, 1939
DeYoung, Harry: San Antonio, 1936
Dobson, Margaret: Kaufman, 1939
Donecker, Fred and Sons: Decatur, San
    Antonio, various sites in central Texas,
    1900s – 1940s
Dozier, Otis: Arlington, Dallas, Fredericksburg,
    Giddings, 1930s – 1940s
Edwards, Ethel: Lampasas, 1940

Edwards, Frank: Ingram, 1946
Fatjo, Arthur: St. Mary's, 1945
Fatjo, Edmund: Shiner, 1954
Faussett, William: Rosenberg, 1941
Finigan, Everett Edwin: San Antonio, 1920s
Fisher, Howard: Liberty, 1939
Flury, Gottfried: Praha, Austin, Hallettsville,
    1880s – 1910s
Frazier, James: San Antonio, 1930s
Fuchs, Fridolin: Westphalia, Lindsay, Muenster,
    1900s – 1910s
Gilboe, Eugene John: Amarillo, Arlington,
    Austin, Brownsville, Dallas, Denton, Fort
    Worth, Galveston, Houston, San Antonio,
    Waco, 1920s – 1940s
Goff, Lloyd: Cooper, 1939
Gonzalez, Xavier: Kilgore, Mission, San
    Antonio, 1930s – 1940s
Grant, Gordon: Brady, 1939
Griewe and Company: San Antonio, 1950s
Hammond, James: Austin, 1930s
Henzel Painting: Mercedes, San Antonio, 1920s
Holmes, Dwight: Fort Worth, date unknown
Hogue, Alexander: Dallas, Graham, Houston,
    1930s – 1940s
Hunter, Warren: Alice, 1939
Hurd, Peter: Big Spring, Dallas, Houston,
    1930s – 1950s
Italian POWs: Umbarger, 1945
Jessen, Harold: Austin, College Station, Goliad,
    1930s
John, Grace Spaulding: Houston, 1939
Keith and Company: Terrill, Kansas City,
    1903 – 1904
Kern, Herman: High Hill, San Antonio, 1910s
Kittelssen, T. J.: El Paso, 1930s
Klepper, Frank: McKinney, 1930s
Knight, Normah: Harlingen, 1940s – 1950s
Laciak, B. E.: Wesley, 1889
Lafayette, A.: Center, 1946
Lea, Tom: Dallas, El Paso, Odessa, Seymour,
    1930s – 1940s

Lester, William: Dallas, 1930s
Levin, Alexander: Jasper, 1939
Lewis, Tom: LaGrange, 1939
Lockwood, Ward: Edinburg, Hamilton, 1940s
Luerssen, Gustav: Lindenau, 1900s – 1910s
Lungkwitz, Herman: Austin, 1880s
Lyon, Nicholas: Conroe, 1938
MacDonnell, Angela: Houston, 1934
MacMorris, Daniel: Houston, Kansas City, 1939
Magafan, Jeanne: Anson, 1941
Maler, W. Kolbe: Weimar, 1890s?
Maragolitti, Vincent: Houston, 1929
Martin, Fletcher: LaMesa, 1940
McAfee, Ila: Clifton, 1941
McBride, H. R.: Austin, 1953
McLeary, Kindred: San Antonio, 1920s
McVey, William: Houston, 1941
Mead, Ben: Canyon, 1934
Mechau, Frank: Brownfield, Fort Worth, 1940
Meister, Charles Martin: Brenham, Houston, 1900 – 1910s
Melchior, Mathias: Warrenton, 1870s
Melchior, Rudolph: Round Top, 1850s – 1860s
Miller, Barse: Baytown, 1938
Mitchel and Halbach: El Paso, 1909
Montag, Camille: Henderson, 1870s
Mozeley, Loren: Alvin, 1940
Netardus, Father _____: Praha, 1900s
Neyland, Watson: Tyrrell, 1934
Nichols, Perry: Dallas, 1930s
Niendorff, Arthur S.: Dallas, 1930s
Ninas, Paul: Henderson, 1937
Oidtman Studios: Fredericksburg, San Antonio, 1930s
Pefferkorn, Father _____: San Antonio, 1896
Pizzi, Pio: East Bernard, 1925
Plotkin, Peter: McKinney, Italy, 1912 – 1915

Raggi, _____: Waco, 1931
Reynolds, Alice: Robstown, 1941
Rollfing, August: Galveston, 1901
Rusca, Louis: Austin, 1907 – 1915
Russell, _____: Palacios, 1900s
Savage, Eugene: Dallas, 1936
Scheuer, Suzanne: Caldwell, Eastland, 1938 – 1939
Schmidt, Julius: Austin, 1907 – 1915
Schnorr, J. Charles: Amarillo, 1930
Smith, Conrad: Austin, 1948
Sokolowski, B. A.: Westphalia, 1895
Starr, Maxwell: Rockdale, 1940s
Stell, Thomas: Teague, 1940
Stockert, Ferdinand: High Hill, San Antonio, 1910s – 1920s
Stone, Ruby: Dallas, 1934
Strong, Ray: Decatur, 1939
Swann, James: Sherman, 1930s
Teichmueller, Minetto: Smithville, 1939
Travis, Olin: Dallas, 1930s – 1940s
Uhler, Ruth Pershing: Houston, 1930s
Van Soelen, Theodore: Livingston, 1940 – 1941
Vitellaro, F. P.: Austin, 1907 – 1915
Walker, John W.: Lockhart, 1939
Weber, August: Serbin, 1870s
Wedmeyer, Henry: San Antonio, 1927
West, Maude: Dallas, 1934
West, Robert: Yoakum, 1894
Wilson, Douthett: Tyler, 1930s
Winn, J. Buck: Dallas, Fort Worth, 1930s
Woeltz, Julius: Amarillo, Elgin, 1939 – 1940
Zakheim, Bernard: Mineola, Rusk, 1938 – 1939
Zell, Mathias: Lindsay, 1919 – 1923
Zografos, John: San Antonio, 1941
Zornes, Milford: El Campo, 1940

Documentation: Patterns and Colors

Pattern sizes and color documentation are provided for interior decorative painting in residential structures over a sixty-year period. This inventory includes the name of the house, the date of decoration, the name of the artist, as well as area, pattern sizes and Munsell colors.

Pattern sizes are included for stencilling, infill painting, and freehand painting where the decorations were easily accessible. Sizes are defined by the subject of the decoration (such as a frieze border or landscape) and by width, length, and height based on placement.

The Munsell Color Code system is used to record color samples. Recognized as an international color language, the method identifies color in a numeric and alphabetic code by hue (color designation), value (lightness or darkness), and intensity or chroma (saturation). Hues are colors like red, yellow, and blue, and are scaled on a ten-point spread with the primary hue placed at five. Values are scaled on a ten-point spread from black (notation N 0/) to white (notation N 10/). Chroma is the degree of difference of a color from the same neutral value of gray outward from one to fourteen. A true yellow, therefore, would be 5Y, with a lighter shade ar 5Y 8.5; a stronger and brighter saturation of yellow — like "yield" signs on highways, for example — is rated at 5Y 8.5/14.

McGregor-Grimm House
Date: ca. 1861 – 1868
Artist: Rudolph Melchior
Area: Entry Hall
Munsell Colors:
Blues (5B 4/4; 5BG 9/2; 7.5BG 8/2)
Golds (5YR 6/2; 10YR 5/6; 7.5YR 3/2; 2.5YR 6/6)
Background (7.5B 7/4)
Area: Parlor
Pattern Sizes:
Floral rinceau: 1' – 6"w repeat × 7"h stencilled
Vase with fruits and flowers — approximately 1' – 6"w × 1' – 6"h, infill painting, freehand painting.
Munsell Colors:
Background: Cream (5Y 8.5/2)
Fruits and flowers (selected code)
Blues (5BG 5/2; 10B 6/4; 5B 8/2; 5B 7/2)
Reds (7.5R 4/10; 7.5R 4/12: 5R 8/2)
Golds (10YR 6/10; 5YR 4/6; 2.5YR 4/6; 5Y 9/2; 2.5Y 7/8; 5Y 6/6; 7.5Y 4/4)
Greens (5GY 5/8; 7.5GY 5/6; 10GY 4/4)

Gluck-Kadernoschka Place
Date: ca. 1860s – 1880s
Area: Bedroom
Landscape with river: 5' – 9"w × 5'h
Landscape with mountains: 3' – 5"w × 5' – 1"h

Knolle-Schroeder House
Date: ca. 1860s – 1890s
Area: Parlor
Pattern Sizes: 7 1/2"w stripe band, 1' – 7"h floral repeat
Munsell Colors:
Background: Dull red (7.5R 4/6)
Dado: Gray (N2.25/)
Patterns (selected code)
Golds (2.5Y 4/4; 10YR 3/2; 2.5Y 5/4)
Reds (10R 3/6; 7.5R 4/6: 10R 4/2)
Blues (2.5B 4/4)

Marburger-Witte House
Date: Before ca. 1900
Area: Parlor
Pattern Sizes:
Decorative border: 1' – 3 1/2"w
Anthemion motifs: 11" repeat × 5"h
Floral rinceau designs: 11"w repeat × 3"h

Eichholt-Guderian-Kruse House
Date: ca. 1902
Artist: Charles Martin Meister
Area: Dining Room
Pattern Sizes:
Center Medallion: 6' – 0"w × 6' – 0"l
Patterned Perimeter Border: 1' – 7"w
Anthemion Motif: 1' – 9"w repeat × 6"h
Munsell Colors:

Yellows and Oranges (5YR 2.5/1; 5YR 3/2;
  10YR 6/10; 2.5YR 3/2; 2.5YR 4/4; 5YR 5/4;
  2.5Y 7/8; 2.5Y 7/10)
Reds (7.5R 6/8; 10R 6/10; 10R 4/8)
Blues (5B 6/4; 7.5B 5/4; 5B 6/2)
Greens (7.5G 3/4; 5G 7/2; 10GY 4/4; 7.5GY 5/6)
Background (5Y 8/2)

Nordt-Dougherty House
Date: ca. 1900 – 1905
Artist: Charles Martin Meister
Area: Entry hall
Pattern Sizes:
Ceiling Medallion: 3' – 10"w × 5' – 7"l
Ceiling Border with Pattern: 2' – 0"w
Ceiling Anthemion Pattern: 1' – 8"w
  repeat × 6"h
Frieze Border: 1' – 9"w repeat × 10"h
Wall Anthemion Pattern: 7"w repeat × 5"h
Munsell Colors:
Background (10GY 7/2)
Blues (5B 6/4; 5B 5/4; 5BG 5/2)
Greens (5G 6/6; 5G 5/6; 5GY 2.5/2)
Reds (7.5R 5/8; 10R 5/8; 5R 3/6; 10R 6/8;
  10R 2.5/2; 10YR 6/8)
Gray (N 8.0/)
Area: Dining Room
Pattern Sizes:
Center Medallion: 7' – 3" diameter
Vase Corner Motif: 1' – 9"w × 1' – 3"h
Munsell Colors:
Background (10GY 7/2)
Reds (10R 4/8; 10R 5/10; 10R 3/4; 10R 5/12)
Yellows and Oranges (7.5YR 6/6; 2.5YR 4/4;
  2.5YR 6/14; 5YR 3/2; 7.5YR 7/6; 5YR 6/10;
  10YR 8/2; 7.5YR 6/10; 10YR 7/8; 10YR 5/6;
  5YR 6/6; 5Y 2.5/1)
Greens (5G 2.5/2; 7.5GY 3/2; 2.5GY 5/6;
  10GY 4/2)
Blues (10BG 6/4; 2.5BG 4/4; 5BG 5/4; 5BG 5/2;
  7.5BG 5/4; 5PB 4/6)
Gray (N 8.0/)

Warren-Crowell House
Date: ca. 1904
Artist: Keith and Company
Area: Parlor
Pattern Sizes:
Top border pattern: 7"w repeat × 6"h
Large frieze pattern: 2' – 4"w repeat × 2' – 5"h
Munsell Colors:
Wall background: Green (2.5GY 4/2)

Curved patterns:
Turquoise blue (2.5BG 4/2)
Brown (10YR 4/6; 7.5YR 4/6)
Yellow gold (10YR 5/4)
Dark green (2.5GY 3/6)
Area: Dining Room
Pattern Sizes:
Pink tulip: 3'w repeat × 3' – 1/2"h (motif with
  yellow spray of flowers is placed on center of
  repeat width)
Munsell Colors:
Wall background: Blue-green (2.50G 5/2)
Leaves and green stripe: Dull green (5GY 4/4)
Pink tulips: Rose (7.5R 5/6 and 7.5R 5/2)
Yellow flowers: Gold (10YR 5/4)
Stripes and swirls: White (N7.0/)
Swirls: Blue (2.5BG 4/2)

Bivins House
Date: ca. 1905
Area: Parlor
Pattern Sizes:
Medallions: approximately 1' – 6" diameter
Art Nouveau scroll motifs: approximately
  1' – 6"w × 3' – 9"h
Squares on ceiling: 2' – 0"w × 2' – 0"l

Harriman-Herlin House
Date: ca. 1905
Artist: Mr. Russell and Mr. Ballard
Area: Upstairs bedroom
Pattern Sizes:
Corner motifs: about 1' – 6"w × 1' – 6"l
Center motifs: about 1' – 6"w × 1' – 3"h
Striped border: about 6"d

Boehm House
Date: ca. 1907
Artist: Gustav Luerssen
Area: Entry hall
Pattern Sizes:
Diamond diaper "wallpaper": 6 1/4"w × 1' –
  4 1/2"h
Ceiling border: 1' – 6"w
Medallion: 2' – 8" diameter
Munsell Colors:
Wall background: Pale gray (N7.25/)
Diamond diaper "wallpaper": Dull rust (2.5YR
  3/4)
Ceiling background: Pale gray (N 7.5/)
Stripe bands on ceiling: Dull green (10G 5/4)
  and muted pink (7.5R 5/2)

Dieringer-Kuester-McChesney House

Date: ca. 1907
Artist: Gustav Luerssen
Area: Parlor
Pattern Sizes:
Diamond diaper "wallpaper": 8 1/4"w × 1' –
    4 1/2"h
Ceiling border: 2' – 8"w
Medallion: 3' – 0" diameter
Munsell Colors:
Wall background: Pale blue-gray (5B 7/2)
Diamond Diaper "wallpaper" — snowflake: Dull
    blue-green (5B 5/4)
Ceiling background: Dark gray (N5.75/)
Corner motifs and medallion: Dull blue (5B 4/4)

Kahlich House

Date: ca. 1907
Artist: Gustav Luerssen
Area: Entry hall
Pattern Size: The pattern is generally double the
    size of that used on the wall in the entry hall
    of the Boehm House, 1' – 2"w × 1' – 6"h.
Munsell Colors: All are the same as those used
    in the entry hall of the Boehm House with the
    addition of a dull green in the pattern area.

Kruppa-Zimmerhanzel House

Date: ca. 1912 – 1915
Artist: Czech painter
Area: Parlor
Pattern Sizes:
#444: 10 3/8"w repeat × 9 5/8"h (frieze), 48
    cents
#431: 10 3/4"w repeat × 2' – 5"h (including
    extended stem, dado), 96 cents
#447: 6 1/2"w repeat × 4"h (ceiling perimeter
    border), 24 cents
Ceiling circle: 8' – 0" diameter
Munsell Colors:
Wall background: Dull pink (5R 5/4)
Frieze and dado patterns #444 and #431:
    Rust-brown (2.5YR 3/4) and light gray
    (N6.01/)
Dado background: Gray-purple (2.5R 5/2)
Perimeter border pattern #447: Rust (10R 3/4)

L. T. Wright House

Date: ca. 1917 – 1920
Artist: Donecker and Sons
Area: Living room
Pattern Sizes:
Vase with flowers: 1' – 0"w × 1' – 5"h (frieze)
Mural with dancers: 7' – 6"w × 3' – 6"h

Decorated Texas Structures

An inventory compiled by place, name of building, date of construction, special features and decorations (when known), artist's name, and date of decoration. Compiled through on-site investigation and from primary and secondary sources.

Abbreviations used in this appendix:
dec.: decorated
fh.: freehand
gr.: graining
inf.: infill
mar.: marbling
sten.: stencilling

Frontier or Early

Residential Structures

Austin (Travis County)
Gault-Fleischer House, ca. 1860s (painted over or destroyed): sten., inf., fh.; artist unknown; dec. ca. 1890s.
Cat Spring (Austin County)
Gluck-Kadernoschka Place, ca. 1860s (some decorations removed): fh.; artist unknown; dec. ca. 1860s – 1880s.
Hess-Kollatschny-Hood House, ca. 1850s: sten.; artist unknown; dec. unknown.
Industry (Austin County)
Hackfield House, ca. 1850s, 1880: sten.; artist unknown; dec. ca. 1900s.
Knolle-Schroeder House, ca. 1868 (painting extant): sten., inf., fh., mar.; artist unknown; dec. after ca. 1868.
Sieper-Knolle-Raeke House, ca. 1850s (painting reproduced or restored): sten., inf.; artist unknown; dec. after ca. 1850s.
Liberty (Liberty County)
Gillard-Duncan House, ca. 1848 – 1850: gr., mar.; artist unknown; dec. unknown.
Round Top (Fayette County)
Biegel House (Winedale), ca. 1832 (partly painted over, new use for building): sten.; artist unknown; dec. unknown.
Jacomini House, ca. 1857: sten., inf.; artist unknown; dec. after ca. 1857.

Lewis House (Winedale), ca. 1850s (new use for building): sten., inf., fh., mar. by Rudolph Melchior, ca. 1850s – 1860s.
Meinecke-Krause House, ca. 1848 – 1856: sten.; artist unknown; dec. before ca. 1865.
Tyler-Goodman House, unknown: sten., inf.; artist unknown; dec. unknown.
Shelby (Austin County)
House on Hwy. 389 N., unknown: sten., gr.; artist unknown; dec. unknown.
Warrenton (Fayette County)
Randall Log House, ca. 1852: sten.; artist unknown; dec. unknown.

Religious Structures

Goliad (Goliad County)
Mission Rosario, unknown: sten., inf., fh. by Harold (Bubi) Jessen (?), ca. 1931.
San Antonio (Bexar County)
Mission Concepcion, ca. 1752, 1955: sten., inf., fh. by F. Stockert (?), unknown.
Mission San Jose, ca. 1768 – 1777 (painting reproduced or restored): sten., inf.; artist unknown; dec. unknown.
San Fernando Cathedral, ca. 1738, 1873: sten., inf., fh.; artist unknown; dec. before ca. 1927.

Greek Revival

Residential Structures

Bastrop (Bastrop County)
Crocheron House, ca. 1857 (painted over): gr.; artist unknown; dec. unknown.
Brenham (Washington County)
Quebe House, ca. 1848: sten., inf., fh. by Charles Meister, ca. 1900 – 1905.
Chappell Hill (Washington County)
Browning Plantation, ca. 1856 – 1858 (painted over): gr.; artist unknown; dec. ca. 1910.

Galveston (Galveston County)
Samuel May Williams House, ca. 1840s (painted over): gr.; artist unknown; dec. after ca. 1840s.
Hempstead (Waller County)
Liendo Plantation, ca. 1853: sten., inf., fh.; artist unknown; dec. after ca. 1853.
Hopewell Community (Titus County)
Rogers-Drummond House, ca. 1854, 1916: sten., inf., mar., gr.; artist itinerant; dec. ca. 1885.
Houston (Harris County)
Nichols-Rice Cherry House, ca. 1845 – 1850 (new use for building): mar. by Mrs. Cherry (?), after ca. 1890s.
Jefferson (Marion County)
House of the Seasons, ca. 1872: sten., inf., fh.; artist unknown; dec. after ca. 1872.
Round Top (Fayette County)
McGregor-Grimm House, ca. 1861 (new use for building): sten., inf., fh., mar., gr. by Rudolph Melchior, ca. 1861 – 1868.
San Augustine (San Augustine County)
Cartwright House, ca. 1840: mar.; artist unknown; dec. unknown.
Warrenton (Fayette County)
Neese House, ca. 1872: sten., inf., fh. by Mathias Melchior, ca. 1870s.
Washington (Washington County)
Hatfield House, ca. 1854: sten.; artist unknown; dec. after ca. 1854.
West Columbia (Brazoria County)
Varner-Hogg Plantation, ca. 1835 (painted over or structure destroyed, new use for building): sten., inf.; artist unknown; dec. before ca. 1901.

Victorian

Residential Structures

Anderson (Grimes County)
Talbot-Moody House, ca. 1880s: sten., inf., fh.; artist unknown; dec. unknown.
Austin (Travis County)
Hirshfeld House, ca. 1886 (new use for building): sten., inf., fh.; artist unknown; dec. unknown.
Paggi House, unknown (painting reproduced or restored, new use for building): sten. (mantels); artist unknown; dec. unknown.
Walter Tips House (now Franklin Savings Assoc.), ca. 1876 (painting reproduced by Buie Harwood and Bill Kurtts, some areas painted over, new use for building): sten., inf., fh.; artist unknown; dec. unknown.

Von Rosenberg House, ca. 1880s (painted over or structure destroyed): sten., inf. by Herman Lungkwitz; dec. unknown.
Beckville (Panola County)
Sterrett House, ca. 1889 (structure destroyed): sten., inf., fh., mar.; artist itinerant; dec. ca. 1889.
Brenham (Washington County)
Eichholt-Guderian-Kruse House, ca. 1865, 1929: sten., inf., fh., gr., mar. by Charles Meister, ca. 1902.
Nordt-Dougherty House, before ca. 1882: sten., inf., fh. by Charles Meister, ca. 1900.
Dallas (Dallas County)
Wilson House, ca. 1898: inf., fh.; artist unknown; dec. after ca. 1898.
Decatur (Wise County)
Waggoner Mansion, ca. 1884: fh. by Fred Donecker, ca. 1900.
Ehlinger (Fayette County)
Kranek-Ehlinger House, ca. 1890s: sten.; artist unknown; dec. unknown.
El Paso (El Paso County)
Magoffin House, ca. 1875 (new use for building): gr.; artist unknown; dec. unknown.
Flatonia (Fayette County)
Faires House, ca. 1880s: sten., inf. by Gottfried Flury, ca. 1895 – 1902.
Gainesville (Cooke County)
Bomar-Davis House, ca. 1890s: artist unknown; dec. ca. 1910.
Galveston (Galveston County)
Borden-Rudy House, ca. 1890s: sten., inf., fh. (floor); artist unknown; dec. ca. 1890s.
Clarke-Jockusch House, ca. 1895: sten., inf.; artist unknown; dec. ca. 1890s (?).
Gresham House (Bishop's Palace), ca. 1893 (new use for building): sten., inf., fh.; artist unknown; dec. unknown.
Sealy House (Open Gates), ca. 1889 (new use for building): sten., inf.; artist unknown; dec. ca. 1914 (?).
Henderson (Rusk County)
Montgomery House, unknown (painted over or structure destroyed): by Camille Montag, unknown.
Poe-Jones-Richardson House, ca. 1840s, 1870 (structure destroyed): sten., inf. by Camille Montag, after ca. 1870s.
Industry (Austin County)
Boelshner House, unknown (painted over or structure destroyed): sten.; artist unknown; dec. unknown.

House on Hwy. 109 N., ca. 1880s (?): sten.;
   artist unknown; dec. unknown.
La Grange (Fayette County)
   Kaulbach-Wilson House, ca. 1869, 1885: mar.
      (mantels); artist unknown; dec. ca. 1885.
Leander (Williamson County)
   Heinatz Homestead, unknown: artist unknown;
      dec. unknown.
Lilac Community (Milam County)
   Graves Homestead, ca. 1870s, 1880: sten., inf.;
      artist unknown; dec. unknown.
Macdona (Bexar County)
   Donecker Residence, unknown: artists the
      Doneckers, 1902 – 1940s.
Marfa (Presidio County)
   Cripple Mill Ranch, ca. 1880s: inf.; artist
      unknown; dec. unknown.
Marshall (Harrison County)
   Hagerty-Harris House, ca. 1889: sten.; artist
      unknown; dec. unknown.
Montgomery (Montgomery County)
   Addison-Gandy House, ca. 1892: gr.; artist
      unknown; dec. ca. 1890s.
   J. F. Davis Cottage, ca. 1851, 1895: gr.; artist
      unknown; dec. ca. 1890s.
Navasota (Grimes County)
   Templeman-Grice House, ca. 1893: sten., inf.,
      fh.; artist unknown; dec. unknown.
New Ulm (Austin County)
   Schuette-Blocker House, ca. 1880s: sten., inf.,
      fh. (floor); artist unknown; dec. unknown.
Orange (Orange County)
   Stark Mansion, unknown: artist unknown; dec.
      unknown.
San Antonio (Bexar)
   Angerstein House, ca. 1880 – 1890s: inf., fh.;
      artist unknown; dec. unknown.
   Burg-Donecker-Mahalia House, ca. 1890s: sten.,
      inf., fh. by the Doneckers, ca. 1922.
   Steves House, ca. 1876 (new use for building);
      sten., inf., fh., gr. by the Doneckers, ca.
      1910 – 1920s.
   Stockert Residence (Hackberry St.), unknown: by
      Ferdinand Stockert, after ca. 1919.
Shelby (Austin County)
   Banker House, unknown: sten.; artist unknown;
      dec. unknown.
   Marburger-Witte House, before ca. 1873, 1900:
      sten., inf.; artist unknown; dec. before ca.
      1900.
Swiss Alp (Fayette County)
   Steinmann House, ca. 1870s: inf.; artist
      unknown; dec. unknown.

Tyler (Smith County)
   Patterson-Umberger House, before ca. 1854,
      1882: sten., fh., gr.; artist unknown; dec.
      unknown.
Weimar (Colorado County)
   Dahse-Halla House, before ca. 1890s: sten, inf.,
      fh., gr. by W. Kolbe Maler, unknown.
   Lange-Chudleigh House, ca. 1890s: sten., inf.,
      gr.; artist unknown; dec. unknown.

Religious Structures

Austin (Travis County)
   St. Mary's Catholic, ca. 1874 – 1884: sten., inf.,
      fh. by Louis Rusca, F. P. Vitellaro, Julius
      Schmidt, ca. 1907 – 1915; sten. by Conrad
      Smith, ca. 1948.
   St. Mary's Catholic Club Room, unknown: artist
      Gottfried Flury, ca. 1880s – 1890s.
Castroville (Medina County)
   St. Louis Catholic, ca. 1850, 1880s (painted
      over): sten., inf., fh. by the Doneckers, ca.
      1902, 1944.
Corpus Christi (Nueces County)
   St. Patrick's Catholic, ca. 1882: fh.; artist
      unknown; dec. ca. 1882.
Czestochowa (Karnes County)
   Nativity of the Blessed Virgin Mary Parish, ca.
      1878 – 1931 (painted over or structure
      destroyed): by Gottfried Flury, ca. 1898.
Dallas (Dallas County)
   St. Matthew's Episcopal, ca. 1874 – 1900
      (painted over or structure destroyed): artist
      unknown; dec. unknown.
Galveston (Galveston County)
   First Presbyterian, ca. 1872 – 1889 (painted
      over): inf.; artist unknown; dec. ca. 1889.
   St. Joseph's Catholic, ca. 1859: sten., inf., fh.;
      artist unknown; dec. after ca. 1900.
   St. Mary's Cathedral, ca. 1848 (painted over):
      sten., inf., fh.; artist unknown; dec. unknown.
Houston (Harris County)
   Annunciation Catholic, ca. 1869, 1881: fh.;
      artist unknown; dec. ca. 1893.
La Grange (Fayette County)
   Sacred Heart Catholic, ca. 1887 (painting saved,
      structure destroyed): sten., inf.; artist unknown;
      dec. unknown.
Palestine (Anderson County)
   First Presbyterian, ca. 1888: sten., inf.; artist
      unknown; dec. unknown.
   Sacred Heart Catholic, ca. 1890 (painting
      reproduced or restored): inf., fh.; artist
      unknown; dec. ca. 1890s.

Praha (Fayette County)

St Mary's Catholic, ca. 1895: sten., inf., fh. by Gottfried Flury (ca. 1895) and Father Netardus (after ca. 1901).

San Antonio (Bexar County)

Sacred Heart Catholic, unknown (structure destroyed): artist unknown; dec. unknown.

St. Joseph's Catholic, ca. 1868 – 1912: sten., inf. by Father Pefferkorn (ca. 1896), Ferdinand Stockert and Herman Kern (ca. 1910), and Griewe and Company (ca. 1955).

St. Marys (Lavaca County)

Church of the Immaculate Conception of the Blessed Virgin Mary, ca. 1896: fh. by Arthur Fatjo, ca. 1945.

Schulenberg (Fayette County)

St. Rose of Lima Parish, ca. 1889: by Anton Benecker, ca. 1896.

Serbin (Lee County)

St. Paul's Lutheran, ca. 1867 – 1871: sten., mar. by August Weber, ca. 1870s.

Wesley (Austin County)

Wesley Brethren, ca. 1866, 1883: sten., inf., fh. by B. E. Laciak, ca. 1889.

Westphalia (Falls County)

Church of the Visitation, ca. 1895 (painted over or structure destroyed): sten., fh. by B. A. Sokolowski (ca. 1895) and Fridolin Fuchs (ca. 1914).

Yoakum (Lavaca County)

St. Joseph's Parish, ca. 1876, 1932 (painted over or structure destroyed): fh. by Robert West, ca. 1894.

Commercial Structures

Austin (Travis County)

Driskill Hotel, ca. 1886 (painted over): sten., inf.; artist unknown; dec. unknown.

Galveston (Galveston County)

Grand Opera House, ca. 1894 (painting status unclear): by August Rollfing, ca. 1901.

Hendley Building, ca. 1859 (new use for building): grn.; artist unknown; dec. unknown.

Georgetown (Williamson County)

Lesesne-Stone-KGTN Bldg., ca. 1884: sten., inf.; artist unknown; dec. unknown.

Hallettsville (Lavaca County)

Courthouse, ca. 1899 (painted over or structure destroyed): sten., inf., fh. by Gottfried Flury, ca. 1899.

Houston (Harris County)

Cotton Exchange Building, ca. 1884, 1907 (painting reproduced or restored, new use for building): sten., inf., fh.; artist unknown; dec. ca. 1907 (?).

Magnolia Brewery Building, ca. 1893 (new use for building): sten., inf.; artist unknown; dec. unknown.

New Braunfels (Comal County)

Old Mill Building, unknown (new use for building): sten.; artist unknown; dec. unknown.

Plaza Hotel, unknown (new use for building): sten.; artist unknown; dec. unknown.

Early 20th Century Vernacular

Residential Structures

Beaumont (Orange County)

McFaddin House, ca. 1900s (new use for building): sten., inf., fh.; unknown Kansas City artist; dec. ca. 1900s.

Brenham (Washington County)

Bockhorn Place, unknown: by Charles Meister, ca. 1904.

Engeling House, unknown (painted over or structure destroyed): by Charles Meister, ca. 1900s.

Jacob Folart House, unknown (painted over or structure destroyed): by Charles Meister, ca. 1900.

Muegge-Winkleman House, ca. 1900s: sten., inf., fh. by Charles Meister, ca. 1900s.

C. H. Sander Mansion, ca. 1900 (structure destroyed): sten., inf., fh. by Charles Meister, ca. 1901.

Schwettmann House, unknown: by Charles Meister, ca. 1900s.

Tegeler House, unknown (some decoration saved, structure destroyed): sten., inf. by Charles Meister, ca. 1900s.

Winkleman House, ca. 1900s (house relocated): sten., inf., fh. by Charles Meister, ca. 1900s.

Bryan (Brazos County)

Wilson-Van Riper-Brock House, ca. 1903: sten., inf., fh.; artist unknown; dec. ca. 1908 – 1910.

Cameron (Milam County)

Jistel House, ca. 1900 – 1910: sten., inf.; artist unknown; dec. unknown.

Cistern (Fayette County)

Kruppa-Zimmerhanzel House, ca. 1910: sten., inf., fh.; unknown Czech artist; dec. ca. 1912.

Mares House, ca. 1910 – 1915: sten., inf., fh.; unknown Czech artist; dec. ca. 1910s.

Psencik House, ca. 1912: sten., inf., fh.; unknown Czech artist; dec. ca. 1912.

Tomecek-Beck House, ca. 1900s: sten., inf., fh.; unknown Czech artist; dec. ca. 1913.

Denton (Denton County)

House at 213 Oak St., ca. 1900s: sten., inf., fh.; artist unknown; dec. unknown.

Houston (Harris County)

O. H. Carlisle House, unknown (content or appearance questionable): by Charles Meister, after ca. 1906.

Diehl House, before ca. 1900 (painting reproduced or restored): fh.; artist unknown; dec. ca. 1900s.

Charles Meister House, ca. 1900s (structure destroyed): sten., inf., fh. by Charles Meister, ca. 1907.

Steele House, ca. 1910s (new use for building): sten., inf., fh.; artist unknown; dec. unknown.

Johnson City (Blanco County)

Lyndon Baines Johnson Boyhood Home, ca. 1901, 1907 (painting reproduced or restored; new use for building): sten., inf.; artist unknown; dec. ca. 1913, 1930s.

Lindenau (Dewitt County)

John Arndt House, ca. 1900s (painted over or structure destroyed): by Gustav Luerssen, ca. 1900s.

Boehm House, before ca. 1893?: sten., inf., mar. by Gustav Luerssen, ca. 1907.

Dieringer-Kuester-McChesney House, ca. 1900s: sten., inf., grn., mar. by Gustav Luerssen, ca. 1907.

Kahlich House, ca. 1907: sten., inf., grn. by Gustav Luerssen, ca. 1900s.

August Olle House, ca. 1900s (painted over or structure destroyed): by Gustav Luerssen, ca. 1900s.

Charlie Schlenstad House, ca. 1900s (painted over or structure destroyed): by Gustav Luerssen, ca. 1900s.

Moulton (Lavaca County)

Jaeggli House, unknown (painted over or structure destroyed): by Gottfried Flury, ca. 1905.

Palacios (Matagorda County)

Harriman-Herlin House, ca. 1905 – 1910: sten., inf., fh. by a Mr. Russell and a Mr. Ballard.

San Antonio (Bexar County)

Donecker House (Cherry St.), unknown: by the Doneckers, ca. 1904.

Donecker House (Montana St.), unknown: by the Doneckers, ca. 1904 – 1909.

Donecker-Hadley House, ca. 1900s: sten., inf., fh. by William Donecker, ca. 1913.

Wichita Falls (Wichita County)

Kell House, ca. 1909: sten., inf. by Theodore Beck, ca. 1919.

Yorktown (Dewitt County)

Otto Roehl House, ca. 1900: sten., inf., fh.; artist unknown; dec. unknown.

Wieland House, unknown (painted over or structure destroyed): sten., inf., fh.; artist unknown; dec. unknown.

Religious Structures

Ammansville (Fayette County)

St. John the Baptist Catholic, ca. 1919: sten., inf., fh., mar. by the Doneckers, ca. 1919.

Beaumont (Orange County)

St. Anthony's Catholic, ca. 1903: artist unknown; dec. ca. 1937.

St Michael's Syrian Orthodox, unknown: sten., inf., fh.; artist unknown; dec.unknown.

Cistern (Fayette County)

St. Cyril and Methodius Catholic, unknown (painted over): sten.; unknown Czech artist; dec. ca. 1911 – 1921.

Clifton (Bosque County)

Trinity Lutheran, ca. 1907: artist unknown; dec. after ca. 1907.

Dallas (Dallas County)

Church of the Sacred Heart, ca. 1902 (painted over or structure destroyed): artist unknown; dec. unknown.

Dubina (Fayette County)

St. Cyril and Methodius Catholic, ca. 1909: sten., inf., fh.; artist unknown; dec. ca. 1909.

Fredericksburg (Gillespie County)

St. Mary's Catholic, ca. 1906: sten., inf., fh., mar., by Fred Donecker (ca. 1906) and Oidtmann Studios (ca. 1936).

High Hill (Fayette County)

St. Mary's Catholic, ca. 1905: sten., inf., fh., mar., by Ferdinand Stockert and Herman Kern, ca. 1912.

Hostyn (Fayette County)

Queen of the Holy Rosary Parish, ca. 1908 (painted over or structure destroyed): inf., fh.; artist unknown; dec. ca. 1908 – 1966.

Lacoste (Medina County)

Our Lady of Grace Catholic, ca. 1911, 1924 (painted over or structure destroyed): sten., inf., fh. by the Doneckers, ca. 1947.

Laredo (Webb County)

St. Peter's Catholic, unknown: artist unknown; dec. ca. 1899.

Lindenau (Dewitt County)
St John's Evangelical Lutheran, unknown
(painted over): Gustav Luerssen, ca. 1900s.
Lindsay (Cooke County)
St. Peter's Catholic, ca. 1918: sten., inf., fh. by
Fridolin Fuchs (ca. 1919) and Mathias Zell
(ca. 1919 – 1923).
Moravia (Lavaca County)
Ascension Catholic, ca. 1913: sten., inf., fh.,
mar., by the Doneckers, ca. 1923.
Moulton (Lavaca County)
St. John's Catholic, unknown (painted over or
structure destroyed): by Gottfried Flury, ca.
1900s.
Muenster (Cooke County)
Sacred Heart Catholic, unknown: sten., inf., fh.
by Fridolin Fuchs, ca. 1906.
Nada (Colorado County)
Nativity of the Blessed Virgin Mary, ca.
1897 – 1901 (painted over or structure
destroyed): artist unknown; dec. ca.
1897 – 1930.
New Braunfels (Comal County)
Sacred Heart Catholic, unknown: by the
Doneckers; dec. unknown.
Refugio (Refugio County)
Our Lady of Refuge, unknown: artist unknown;
dec. ca. 1905.
Rosenberg (Fort Bend County)
Holy Rosary Catholic, ca. 1911 – 1924 (painted
over or structure destroyed): artist unknown;
dec. ca. 1911.
Shiner (Lavaca County)
St. Cyril and Methodius Catholic, ca. 1919:
sten., fh. by Edmond Fatjo, ca. 1950s.
Sweet Home (Lavaca County)
Church of the Blessed Virgin Mary, ca. 1919:
sten., fh., mar. by the Doneckers, ca. 1919.
Wallis (Austin County)
Church of the Guardian Angel, ca. 1913
(painting reproduced or restored): sten., inf.,
fh.; unknown immigrant artists (ca. 1913),
redone by unknown German artists (ca.
1960s).

Commercial Structures

Houston (Harris County)
Macatee Hotel, ca. 1906 – 1960 (painted over or
structure destroyed): sten., inf., fh.; artist
unknown; dec. ca. 1906.
Richmond (Fort Bend County)
Dance Hall (Arroyo Seco Park), ca. 1900s (new

use for building): sten., inf., fh.; artist
unknown; dec. unknown.
San Antonio (Bexar County)
Southern Pacific Train Station, ca. unknown
(painted over): by the Doneckers; dec.
unknown.

Arts and Crafts or Prairie

Residential Structures

El Paso (El Paso County)
Henry Trost House, ca. 1906 – 1909: sten., by
Mitchel and Halbach, ca. 1909.
San Antonio (Bexar County)
L.T. Wright House, ca. 1917 (new use for
building): sten., inf., fh. by the Doneckers, ca.
1917 – 1920.
Terrell (Kaufman County)
Warren-Crowell House, ca. 1903 – 1904: sten.,
inf., fh. by Keith and Co., ca. 1903 – 1904.

Colonial or Classical Revival

Residential Structures

Amarillo (Potter County)
Bivins House, ca. 1904 – 1905 (new use for
building): sten., inf., fh.; artist unknown; dec.
unknown.
Landergin-Harrington House, ca. 1913 – 1915
(new use for building): sten., inf., fh.; artist
unknown; dec. unknown.
Fort Worth (Tarrant County)
Wharton-Scott House (Thistle Hill), ca. 1904
(new use for building): sten., inf. fh.; artist
unknown; dec. unknown.
Gonzales (Gonzales County)
Dilworth-Clemons House, ca. 1910: sten., inf.,
fh.; unknown Viennese artist; dec. unknown.
McKinney (Collin County)
Burton-Merritt House, ca. 1905: sten., inf., fh.
by Peter Plotkin, ca. 1912 – 1915.
Vernon (Wilbarger County)
W. D. Berry House, ca. 1906 (new use for
building): sten., inf., fh. by Mr. Beck (?); dec.
ca. 1925.

Commercial Structures

Austin (Travis County)
Majestic-Paramount Theater, ca. 1915 (painting
reproduced or restored): sten, inf., fh.; artist
unknown; dec. ca. 1930.
University of Texas-Battle Hall Library, ca. 1910:
sten, inf., fh.; artist unknown; dec. unknown.

Dallas (Dallas County)

Adolphus Hotel, ca. 1912 (painted over or
structure destroyed): fh. by Eugene Gilboe,
dec. unknown.

City Hall, ca. 1914 (painted over): fh. by Jerry
Bywaters and Alexander Hogue, ca. 1934.

Galveston (Galveston County)

City National Bank (now Galveston County
Historical Museum), ca. 1919: sten., inf., fh.;
artist unknown; dec. ca. 1919?

Port Isabel (Cameron County)

Champion Store and Restaurant, ca. 1900s (new
use for building): fh.; artist unknown; dec.
unknown.

Revival Influences

Residential Structures

Dallas (Dallas County)

King Mansion, ca. 1920s (painted over): fh. by
Jacques Carlew, dec. unknown.

San Antonio (Bexar County)

Landa House (now the Landa Library), ca. 1928:
sten., inf., fh. by Kindred McLeary, after ca.
1928.

Luchesse-Walker House, ca. 1926: fh. by Frank
Cloonan, unknown.

McNay Residence (now the McNay Art
Museum), ca. 1927 (new use for building):
sten., inf., fh.; artist unknown; dec. ca. 1927.

Religious Structures

Amarillo (Potter County)

First Baptist Church, ca. 1930: sten., inf., fh. by
J. Charles Schnorr, ca. 1930.

Brownsville (Cameron County)

Immaculate Conception Cathedral, unknown
(painted over or structure destroyed), artist
unknown; dec. unknown.

Columbus (Colorado County)

Smith-Grates Chapel, ca. 1920s – 1930 (question
on some content or appearance): artist
unknown; dec. unknown.

East Bernard (Wharton County)

Parish of the Holy Cross, unknown: sten., fh. by
Pio Pizzi, ca. 1925.

Fort Worth (Tarrant County)

St. Demetrius Greek Orthodox, unknown: fh.;
artist unknown, dec. unknown.

Houston (Harris County)

Villa De Matel, unknown: sten., inf., fh.; artist
unknown; dec. unknown.

Paris (Lamar County)

First United Methodist, ca. 1922: sten., inf., fh.,;
artist unknown; dec. unknown.

San Angelo (Tom Green County)

Assumption of the Virgin Mary Greek Orthodox,
unknown: fh., artist unknown; dec. after ca.
1937.

San Antonio (Bexar County)

Our Lady of the Lake Chapel, ca. 1921: sten.,
inf., fh. by Oidtmann Studios, ca. 1935.

St. Francis of Paola, unknown: sten.; artist
unknown; dec. before ca. 1927.

St. Mary's Catholic, ca. 1924: sten., inf., fh. by
Oidtmann Studios, ca. 1936.

St. Sophia Greek Orthodox, ca. 1926: inf., fh.
(icons on walls) by John Zografos (ca. 1927,
1941).

Umbarger (Randall County)

St. Mary's Catholic, ca. 1930: sten., inf., fh. by
Italian POWs, ca. 1945.

Victoria (Victoria Parish)

Our Lady of Lourdes Parish, ca. 1923: sten.,
inf., fh.; artist unknown; dec. ca. 1924.

Waco (McLennan County)

Church of St. Francis, ca. 1931: fh. by Raggi,
ca. 1931.

Yorktown (Dewitt County)

Holy Cross Parish, unknown: artist unknown;
dec. unknown.

Commercial Structures

Amarillo (Potter County)

Capitol Hotel, unknown (question on some
content or appearance): sten., inf., fh. by J.
Charles Schnorr, unknown.

Arlington (Tarrant County)

Arlington Theater, unknown (question on some
content or appearance): fh. by Eugene Gilboe,
unknown.

Austin (Travis County)

Austin Public Library, ca. 1933: sten., inf., fh.
by Harold (Bubi) Jessen and Peter Allidi, ca.
1933.

Swift-Day Building, unknown (new use for
building, painting reproduced and restored by
Buie Harwood): fh.; artist unknown; dec. ca.
1930s.

University of Texas, Architecture Building (now
Goldsmith Hall), ca. 1932 (reproduced and
restored by Betty McKee Treanor): sten., inf.,
fh. by Peter Allidi, Harold (Bubi) Jessen,
James Hammond and a Mr. Rolfe, ca. 1932.

University of Texas, Chemistry Building (now Welch Hall), ca. 1929 (painting reproduced and restored by Buie Harwood and Betty McKee Treanor): sten., inf., fh.,; artist unknown; dec. ca. 1930s.

University of Texas, Library (now Main Building), ca. 1932 – 1937: sten., inf., fh. by Eugene Gilboe, ca. 1933.

University of Texas, Student Union, ca. 1932 (painted over): sten., inf., fh. by Eugene Gilboe, ca. 1932.

Ballinger (Runnels County)

Lynn-Hathaway Building, unknown: artist unknown, dec. unknown.

Canyon (Randall County)

Panhandle Plains Museum, ca. 1930s: fh. by Ben Mead and Harold Bugbee, ca. 1934.

College Station (Brazos County)

Texas A&M University, Main Building, unknown: fh., by Harold (Bubi) Jessen, ca. 1933.

Dallas (Dallas County)

Boude Storey Jr. High School, ca. 1930s (painted over or structure destroyed): fh. by William Lester, ca. 1930s.

Crozier Technical High School, ca. 1930: fh. by Perry Nichols, ca. 1930s.

Forest Avenue High School, ca. 1930s (painted over or structure destroyed): fh. by Otis Dozier, ca. 1930s.

Hall of Texas Cattle Kings, unknown (question on some content or appearance): fh. by Harold Bugbee, ca. 1937.

Highland Park Town Hall, ca. 1930s (painted over or structure destroyed): fh. by Ruby Stone and Maude West, ca. 1934.

Majestic Theater, ca. 1921 (painted over, later reproduced or restored): fh. by Eugene Gilboe, ca. 1948.

Oak Cliff High School, ca. 1930s (painted over or structure destroyed): fh. by Harry Carnohan, ca. 1930s.

Parkland Hospital, ca. 1930s (painted over): fh. by Adele Brunet, ca. 1930s.

Post office and courthouse, unknown: map of Dallas, artist unknown, ca. 1929; map of Texas, artist unknown, ca. 1929; stencilling on ceiling, artist unknown; dec. unknown.

Stoneleigh Hotel, ca. 1920s – 1930 (painting altered): fh. by Eugene Gilboe, ca. 1935.

Village Theater, ca. 1931: sten., fh. by J. Buck Winn and Reveau Bassett, ca. 1931.

Washington Theater, ca. 1915 – 1932 (painted over or structure destroyed): artist unknown; dec. unknown.

Woodrow Wilson High School, ca. 1930s (painted over or structure destroyed): fh. by William Lester, ca. 1930s.

Delphi (Bastrop County)

Schoolhouse, unknown: sten.; artist unknown; dec. unknown.

El Paso (El Paso County)

Cortez Hotel, ca. 1926: sten., inf., fh.; artist unknown; dec. unknown.

County courthouse, unknown: fh. by T. J. Kittelssen, ca. 1930s.

Federal courthouse, unknown: fh. by Tom Lea, ca. 1936.

Fort Worth (Tarrant County)

Blackstone Hotel, unknown (painted over): fh. by J. Buck Winn, ca. 1930s.

Elks Lodge (now the YWCA), ca. 1928: sten.; artist unknown; dec. ca. 1928.

Main post office, ca. 1930s: mural, Conestoga wagons (3' – 0"w × 3' – 0"h), by Dwight Holmes; landscape with wagons (8' – 0"w × 3' – 0"h), by W. Baker; western town scene (3' – 0"w × 3' – 0"h), by W. Baker; old planes on runway (3' – 0"w × 3' – 0"h), by Dwight Holmes; ship dock scene (8' – 0"w × 3' – 0"h), by Dwight Holmes; farm scene (3' – 0"w × 3' – 0"h), by W. Baker; all dated ca. 1933.

Houston (Harris County)

Esperson Building, ca. 1928: fh. by Eugene Gilboe, ca. 1935.

Franklin Bank, ca. 1920s (painting reproduced or restored): sten., inf.; artist unknown; dec. ca. 1920s.

Public library (Texas Collection), ca. 1926: fh. by Angela MacDonnell (ca. 1934), Ruth P. Uhler (ca. 1935) and E. R. Cherry (ca. 1936).

Mercedes (Hidalgo County)

Hidalgo County Bank, ca. 1927: sten., inf., by Henzel Painting, ca. 1928.

Pampa (Gray County)

Post office, ca. 1930s; sten.; artist unknown; dec. ca. 1934.

Paris (Lamar County)

Carnegie Library, ca. 1930s: fh. by Jerry Bywaters, ca. 1930s.

San Antonio (Bexar County)

Casino Building, ca. 1926 (painted over or structure destroyed): fh. by Henry Wedmeyer, ca. 1927.

Margil Elementary School, ca. 1930s – 1955
(painted over or structure destroyed): fh. by
unknown school children, ca. 1937.
Municipal Auditorium, ca. 1930s (painted over
or structure destroyed): fh. by Xavier
Gonzalez, ca. 1930s.
St. Anthony Hotel, unknown (painted over):
sten., by Everett E. Finigan (ca. 1920s), fh. by
James Frazier (ca. 1930s) and Harry A.
DeYoung and others (ca. 1936).
Thomas Jefferson High School, ca. 1929 – 1932:
sten., inf., fh.; artist unknown; dec. ca. 1930s.
Seguin (Guadalupe County)
Texas Theater, ca. 1929: fh; artist unknown; dec.
ca. 1929.
Sherman (Grayson County)
Sherman Public Library, unknown: fh. by James
Swann, ca. 1930s.
Tyler (Smith County)
Carnegie Library, unknown: fh. by Douthett
Wilson, ca. 1930s.
Tyrrell (Liberty County)
Public library, unknown: fh. by Watson Neyland,
ca. 1934.
Waco (McClennan County)
Baylor University, Browning Library, unknown:
sten., fh., artist unknown; dec. unknown.

Regional

Residential Structures

Dallas (Dallas County)
Miller House, ca. 1930s: fh. by owner, ca.
1930s.
Dickinson (Galveston County)
Kemper-Adeau-Bagat House, ca. 1930s: sten.;
artist unknown; dec. ca. 1930s.
Houston (Harris County)
H. Lawrence Williams House, unknown
(question on some content or appearance): fh.
by Frederick Brown, ca. 1936.
Ingram (Kerr County)
Frank Edwards House, ca. 1940s: fh. by Frank
Edwards, ca. 1946.
San Antonio (Bexar County)
Lutcher-Brown House, ca. 1935 (new use for
building): fh.; artist unknown; dec. unknown.

Art Deco

Commercial Structures

Dallas (Dallas County)
State of Texas Building (now Hall of State), ca.
1935 – 1936: fh. by Eugene Savage, George

Davidson, J. Buck Winn, Tom Lea, Jerry
Bywaters, Olin Travis, Arthur S. Neindorff
and others, ca. 1936.
Transportation Institute, ca. 1936 (structure
destroyed): fh. by F. J. Boerder, ca. 1936.
Fort Worth (Tarrant County)
Texas and Pacific Building, ca. 1931: fh.; artist
unknown; dec. ca. 1930s.
Harlingen (Cameron County)
Holsum-Buttercrust Baking Company, ca. 1930s:
fh. by Normah Knight, ca. 1948.
Houston (Harris County)
City Hall, ca. 1937 – 1939: sten., inf., fh. by
Daniel MacMorris, Ruth P. Uhler and Grace
S. John, ca. 1939.
Gulf Building, ca. 1929 (new use for building):
fh. by Vincent Maragolitti, ca. 1929.
San Antonio (Bexar County)
Aztec Theater, ca. 1927: sten., inf., fh.; artist
unknown; dec. unknown.
Majestic Theater, ca. 1928 – 1929 (painting
reproduced or restored): fh. by Eugene Gilboe,
ca. 1929.
Texas Theater, ca. 1926 (painted over): fh. by
Jose Arpa (ca. 1926) and B. H. Brage (ca.
1928).

*Municipal and Federal Buildings. (Unless otherwise
noted, all the structures are federal post offices, and all
were constructed within a few years of decoration.)*

Alice (Jim Wells County)
Painting, South Texas panorama (12 – 0'w
× 4' – 8"h, painting sent to Smithsonian
Institution, building now a doctor's office), by
Warren Hunter, 1939.
Alpine (Brewster County)
Painting, Alpine, by Jose Moya del Pino, 1940.
Alvin (Brazoria County)
Painting, pioneers (12' – 0"w × 7' – 0"h,
painting extant, structure destroyed), by Loren
Mozeley, 1940.
Amarillo (Potter County)
Painting, cattle loading (room: 18' – 0"
× 30' – 0"), by Julius Woeltz, 1940.
Painting, cattle branding, by Julius Woeltz, 1940.
Painting, oil drilling, by Julius Woeltz, 1940.
Painting, Coronado's exploration party in Palo
Duro Canyon, by Julius Woeltz, 1940.
Painting, gang plow, by Julius Woeltz, 1940.
Painting, Dick Harrow, by Julius Woeltz, 1940.
Anson (Jones County)
Painting, cowboy dance (11' – 9"w ×
7' – 11"h), by Jeanne Magafan, 1941.

Arlington (Tarrant County)

Painting, gathering pecans
(12′w – 0″ × 4′ – 0″h, building now a school
district tax office) by Otis Dozier, 1941.

Baytown (Chambers County)

Fresco, transportation (11′ – 4″w × 6′ – 2″h), by
Barse Miller, 1938.

Big Spring (Howard County)

Painting, pioneers (23 – 0′w × 6′ – 0″h,
building now a library), by Peter Hurd, 1938.

Borger (Hutchinson County)

Painting, big city news (8′ – 10″w × 4′ – 0″h,
painting extant, building now a museum), by
Jose Aceves, 1939.

Brady (McCulloch County)

Painting, Texas immigrant (11′ – 11″w ×
4′ – 1″h), by Gordon Grant, 1939.

Brownfield (Terry County)

Painting, Panhandle ranchers fighting prairie fire
with skinned steer (12′ – 0″w × 5′ – 0″h,
building now a police station), by Frank
Mechau, 1940.

Caldwell (Burleson County)

Painting, Indians moving (12′ – 3″w ×
5′ – 0″h), by Suzanne Scheuer, 1939.

Canyon (Randall County)

Painting, strays (12′ – 8″w × 3′ – 10″h) by
Francis Ankrom, 1938.

Center (Shelby County)

Painting, logging scene (11′ – 10″w × 5′ – 2″h),
by Edward Chavez, 1941.

Clifton (Bosque County)

Painting, longhorns (11′ – 8″w × 4′ – 10″h), by
Ila McAfee, 1941.

College Station (Brazos County)

Painting, good harvest (11′ – 9″w × 5′ – 0″h,
paint status unclear), by Victor Arnautoff,
1938.

Conroe (Montgomery County)

Painting, early Texans (painting relocated or
destroyed), by Nicholas Lyon, 1938.

Cooper (Delta County)

Painting, before the fencing of Delta County
(9′ – 6″w × 5′ – 9″h), by Lloyd Goff, 1939.

Corpus Christi (Nueces County)

Painting, seaport activities (17′ – 2″w ×
4′ – 2″h, painting extant, structure destroyed),
by Howard Cook, 1941.

Painting, agriculture (17′ – 2″w × 4′ – 2″h,
painting extant, structure destroyed), by
Howard Cook, 1941.

Dallas (Dallas County)

Painting, pioneer home builders, by Peter Hurd,

1940; painting, air mail over Texas, by Peter
Hurd, 1940 (building now called the Terminal
Annex).

Decatur (Wise County)

Painting, Texas plains (framed) by Ray Strong,
1939.

Eastland (Eastland County)

Painting, Indian buffalo hunt (12′ – 0″w ×
5′ – 6″h), by Suzanne Scheuer, 1938.

Edinburg (Hidalgo County)

Painting, harvest in the Rio Grande Valley, by
Ward Lockwood, 1940 (building now a bank).

El Campo (Wharton County)

Painting, landscape (question on some content or
appearance), by Milford Zornes, 1940.

Elgin (Bastrop County)

Painting, Texas farm (11′ – 9″w × 6′ – 6″h), by
Julius Woeltz, 1939.

El Paso (El Paso County)

Painting, Pass of the North, by Tom Lea, 1938.

Farmersville (Collin County)

Painting, soil conservation in Collin County
(11′ – 10″w × 6′ – 10″h), by Jerry Bywaters,
1941.

Fort Worth (Tarrant County)

Courthouse: Painting, Sam Bass (11′ – 4″w ×
8′ – 0″h), by Frank Mechau, 1940; painting,
Texas Rangers (11′ – 5″w × 8′ – 0″h), by
Frank Mechau, 1940.

Fredericksburg (Gillespie County)

Painting, loading cattle (11′ – 10″w × 5′ – 2″h),
by Otis Dozier, 1942.

Gatesville (Coryell County)

Painting, off to northern markets (10′ – 0″w ×
5′ – 2″h), by Joe DeYong, 1939.

Giddings (Lee County)

Painting, cowboys receiving the mail
(11′ – 0″w × 4′ – 0″h) by Otis Dozier, 1939.

Graham (Young County)

Painting, Graham oil fields (11′ – 6″w ×
6′ – 8″h), by Alexander Hogue, 1939.

Henderson (Rusk County)

Painting, local industries (painted over or
structure destroyed), by Paul Ninas, 1937.

Hamilton (Hamilton County)

Painting, Texas Rangers (11′ – 0″w × 5′ – 9″h,
painting reproduced or restored), by Ward
Lockwood, 1942.

Houston (Harris County)

Federal courthouse: Painting, Houston ship
channel, by Alexander Hogue, 1941; Painting,
Houston ship canal, by Jerry Bywaters, 1941
(both paintings extant, structure destroyed);

Painting, Battle of San Jacinto (current location of painting unclear), by William McVey, 1941.

Jasper (Jasper County)
Painting, industries of Jasper (6' – 9"w × 4' – 11"h), by Alexander Levin, 1939.

Kaufman (Kaufman County)
Painting, driving steers (painted over or structure destroyed), by Margaret Dobson, 1939.

Kenedy (Karnes County)
Painting, grist for the mill (13' – 10"w × 6' – 1"h), by Charles Campbell, 1939.

Kilgore (Gregg County)
Painting, drilling for oil (15' – 9"w × 5' – 11"h), by Xavier Gonzalez, 1941; Painting, pioneer saga (15' – 9"w × 5' – 11"h); Painting, music of the plains (cut out); Painting, contemporary youth.

LaGrange (Fayette County)
Painting, horses (9' – 9"w × 4' – 0"h), by Tom Lewis, 1939.

Lamesa (Dawson County)
Federal Building: Painting, horse breakers (13' – 0"w × 3' – 7"h), by Fletcher Martin, 1940.

Lampasas (Lampasas County)
Painting, afternoon on a Texas ranch (11' – 10"w × 4' – 0"h), by Ethel Edwards, 1940.

Liberty (Liberty County)
Painting, the big fish (14' – 0"w × 5' – 9"h), by Howard Fisher, 1939.

Linden (Cass County)
Painting, cotton pickers (10' – 9"w × 4' – 7"h), by Victor Arnautoff, 1936 (?).

Livingston (Polk County)
Landscape mural (33' – 10"w × 7' – 0"h, new use for building, now a police station), by Theodore Van Soelen, 1941; Painting, buffalo hunting (11' – 10"w × 6' – 0"h), by Theodore Van Soelen, 1940.

Lockhart (Caldwell County)
Painting, pony express station (10' – 6"w × 4' – 6"h), by John W. Walker, 1939.

Mart (McLennan County)
Painting, McLennan looking for a home (12' – 0"w × 5' – 1"h), by Jose Aceves, 1939.

McKinney (Collin County)
Painting, 3 panels, by Frank Klepper, 1930s.

Mineola (Wood County)
Painting, new and old transportation (13' – 0"w × 5' – 6"h), by Bernard Zakheim, 1938.

Mission (Hidalgo County)
Painting, cowboy in the West Texas plains (13' – 1"w × 4' – 4"h), by Xavier Gonzalez, 1942.

Odessa (Ector County)
Painting, stampede (15' – 4"w × 5' – 5"h), by Tom Lea, 1940.

Quanah (Hardeman County)
Painting, naming of Quanah (13' – 9"w × 4' – 6"h) by Jerry Bywaters, 1938.

Ranger (Eastland County)
Painting, crossroads town (11' – 10"w × 4' – 8"h), by Emil Bisttram, 1939.

Robstown (Nueces County)
Painting, founding and development of Robstown (14' – 0"w × 4' – 6"h), by Alice Reynolds, 1941.

Rockdale (Milam County)
Painting, industry in Rockdale (11' – 10"w × 8' – 0"h), by Maxwell Starr.

Rosenberg (Fort Bend County)
Painting, LaSalle's last expedition (mural relocated), by William Faussett, 1941.

Rusk (Cherokee County)
Painting, agriculture and industry (11' – 4"w × 3' – 5"h), by Bernard Zakheim, 1939.

San Antonio (Bexar County)
Fresco, San Antonio's importance in Texas history (16 panels that vary in size), by Howard Cook, 1937 (building now known as the Downtown Station).

Seymour (Baylor County)
Painting, Comanches (13' – 6"w × 4' – 10"h), by Tom Lea, 1942.

Smithville (Bastrop County)
Painting, Texas Rangers (11' – 10"w × 5' – 2"h), by Minetto Teichmueller, 1939.

Teague (Freestone County)
Painting, cattle roundup, (8' – 1"w × 3' – 2"h), by Thomas Stell, Jr., 1940.

Trinity (Trinity County)
Painting, lumber manufacturing (11' – 0"w × 4' – 2"h), by Jerry Bywaters, 1942.

Wellington (Collingsworth County)
Painting, Collingsworth County settlers (12' – 9"w × 5' – 6"h), by Bernard Arnest, 1939.

1940s – 1950s Post War

Theaters

Amarillo (Potter County)
Esquire Theater, ca. 1948: sten., fh. by Eugene Gilboe, ca. 1948.

Austin (Travis County)
  Burnet Road Drive-In Theater, ca. 1953: fh. by
    H. R. McBride, ca. 1953.
  Chief Drive-In Theater, ca. 1953: fh. by H. R.
    McBride, ca. 1953.
Brownsville (Cameron County)
  Majestic Theater, ca. 1949: sten., fh. by Eugene
    Gilboe, ca. 1949.
Dallas (Dallas County)
  Circle Theater, ca. 1947 (painting altered): fh. by
    Eugene Gilboe, ca. 1947.
  Esquire Theater, ca. 1947 (painting altered): fh.
    by Eugene Gilboe, ca. 1947.
  Forest Theater, ca. 1949 (painting altered): fh. by
    Eugene Gilboe, ca. 1949.
  Inwood Theater, ca. 1947: sten., inf., fh. by
    Eugene Gilboe, ca. 1947.
  Lakewood Theater, unknown, by Eugene
    Gilboe, dec. unknown.
  Melba Theater, unknown (question on some
    content or appearance): by Eugene Gilboe,
    dec. unknown.
  Melrose Theater, unknown (question on some
    content or appearance): by Eugene Gilboe,
    dec. unknown.
  Mercantile Bank Building, unknown: by Eugene
    Gilboe, dec. unknown.
  Palace Theater, ca. 1952 (painted over or
    structure destroyed): fh. by Eugene Gilboe, ca.
    1952.
  Tower Theater, ca. 1951 (painted over or
    structure destroyed): fh. by Eugene Gilboe, ca.
    1951.
  Wilshire Theater, ca. 1946 (painted over or
    structure destroyed): fh. by Eugene Gilboe, ca.
    1946.
Denton (Denton County)
  Campus Theater, ca. 1949: fh. by Eugene
    Gilboe, ca. 1949.
Fort Worth (Tarrant County)
  Ridglea Theater, ca. 1950: fh. by Eugene
    Gilboe, ca. 1950.

Galveston (Galveston County)
  Broadway Theater, ca. 1947 (painting altered):
    sten., fh. by Eugene Gilboe, ca. 1947.
Houston (Harris County)
  Fulton Theater, ca. 1947 (question on some
    content or appearance): fh. by Eugene Gilboe,
    ca. 1947.
  Garden Oaks Theater, ca. 1947: sten., inf., fh.
    by Eugene Gilboe, ca. 1947.
  Santa Rosa Theater, ca. 1947: sten., fh. by
    Eugene Gilboe, ca. 1947.
  Tower Theater, ca. 1947 (painting altered): fh. by
    Eugene Gilboe, ca. 1947.
Waco (McClennan County)
  25th Street Theater, unknown (painting altered):
    fh. by Eugene Gilboe, unknown.

Commercial Structures

Brownsville (Cameron County)
  Texas Cafe (Market Square), unknown: fh. by
    Antonio Cisneros, ca. 1940s.
Center (Shelby County)
  Parker Brothers Motor Company, ca. 1945: fh.
    by A. Lafayette, ca. 1946.
College Station (Brazos County)
  Texas A&M University, Agricultural Engineering
    Building, unknown: fh. by Gertrude Babcock,
    ca. 1940.
Dallas (Dallas County)
  Baker Hotel, unknown (painted over or structure
    destroyed): fh. by Eugene Gilboe, ca. 1947.
Harlingen (Cameron County)
  First National Bank, ca. 1951 (painting extant,
    relocated to post office): fh. by Normah
    Knight, ca. 1951.
Houston (Harris County)
  Prudential Insurance (University of Texas, M. D.
    Anderson Hospital), ca. 1952: fh. by Peter
    Hurd, ca. 1952.

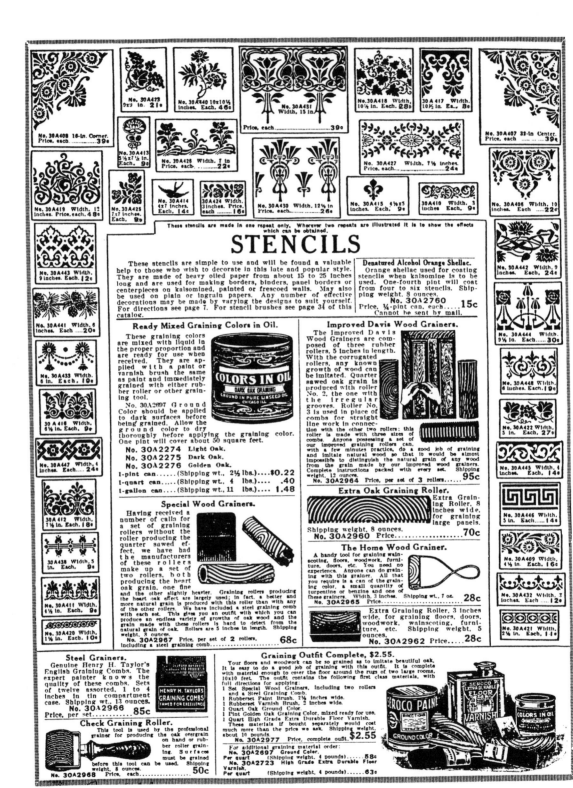

Stencil illustrations (clockwise from upper left):

No. 30A443 9x9 in. 21c
No. 30A440 10x10¼ inches. Each. 46c
No. 30A431 Width, 15 in. Price, each 39c
No. 30A418 Width, 10½ in. Each. 28c
No. 30A417 Width. 10½ in. Ea. 8c
No. 30A408 16-in. Corner. Price, each. 39c
No. 30A407 22-in. Center. Price, each. 39c
No. 30A413 5½x7½ in. Each. 9c
No. 30A426 Width, 7 in. Price, each. 22c
No. 30A427 Width. 7½ in. Price, each. 24c
No. 30A419 Width, 12 inches. Price, each, 48c
No. 30A425 7x7 inches. Each, 9c
No. 30A414 4x7 inches. Each, 14c
No. 30A424 Width, 3 inches. Price, each 16c
No. 30A430 Width, 12½ in Price, each 26c
No. 30A415 4½x5 inches. Each, 9c
No. 30A410 Width, 3 inches. Each, 9c
No. 30A406 Width, 10 inches. Each 22c
No. 30A442 Width, 9 inches. Each, 24c
No. 30A444 Width, 9½ in. Each. 30c
No. 30A448 Width, 6 inches. Each. 19c
No. 30A422 Width, 5 in. Each. 27c
No. 30A445 Width, 5 inches. Each. 14c
No. 30A446 Width, 5 in. Each. 14c
No. 30A409 Width. 4½ in. Each. 16c
No. 30A432 Width, 7 inches. Each. 12c
No. 30A421 Width, 2½ in. Each. 11c
No. 30A443 Width, 9 inches. Each. 12c
No. 30A441 Width, 6 inches. Each. 20c
No. 30A433 Width, 8 in. Each. 19c
No. 30A416 Width, 6½ in. Each. 9c
No. 30A447 Width, 4 inches. Each. 24c
No. 30A412 Width, 7½ in. Each. 18c
No. 30A438 Width, 5 in. Each. 9c
No. 30A411 Width, 4½ in. Each. 9c
No. 30A420 Width, 1¼ in. Each. 10c

These stencils are made in one repeat only. Wherever two repeats are illustrated it is to show the effects which can be obtained.

STENCILS

These stencils are simple to use and will be found a valuable help to those who wish to decorate in this late and popular style. They are made of heavy oiled paper from about 15 to 25 inches long and are used for making borders, binders, panel borders or centerpieces on kalsomined, painted or frescoed walls. May also be used on plain or ingrain papers. Any number of effective decorations may be made by varying the designs to suit yourself. For directions see page 7. For stencil brushes see page 34 of this catalog.

Denatured Alcohol Orange Shellac.

Orange shellac used for coating stencils when kalsomine is to be used. One-fourth pint will coat from four to six stencils. Shipping weight, 8 ounces.
No. 30A2760
Price, ¼-pint can, each..... 15c
Cannot be sent by mail.

Ready Mixed Graining Colors in Oil.

These graining colors are mixed with liquid in the proper proportion and are ready for use when received. They are applied with a paint or varnish brush the same as paint and immediately grained with either rubber roller or other graining tool.

COLORS IN OIL — DARK OAK GRAINING — GROUND IN PURE LINSEED OIL — CHICAGO ILL.

No. 30A2697 Ground Color should be applied to dark surfaces before being grained. Allow the ground color to dry thoroughly before applying the graining color. One pint will cover about 50 square feet.

No. 30A2274 Light Oak.
No. 30A2275 Dark Oak.
No. 30A2276 Golden Oak.
1-pint can...... (Shipping wt., 2½ lbs.).....$0.22
1-quart can..... (Shipping wt., 4 lbs.).... .40
1-gallon can.... (Shipping wt., 11 lbs.)..... 1.48

Special Wood Grainers.

Having received a number of calls for a set of graining rollers without the roller producing the quarter sawed effect, we have had the manufacturers of these rollers make up a set of two rollers, both producing the heart oak grain, one fine and the other slightly heavier. Graining rollers producing the heart oak effect are largely used; in fact, a better and more natural grain is produced with this roller than with any of the other rollers. We have included a steel graining comb with each set. This gives you an outfit with which you can produce an endless variety of growths of oak wood and the grain made with these rollers is hard to detect from the natural grain of oak. Rollers are 5 inches in length. Shipping weight, 8 ounces.
No. 30A2967 Price, per set of 2 rollers, including a steel graining comb. 68c

Improved Davis Wood Grainers.

The Improved Davis Wood Grainers are composed of three rubber rollers, 5 inches in length. With the corrugated rollers, any known growth of wood can be imitated. Quarter sawed oak grain is produced with roller No. 2, the one with the irregular grooves. Roller No. 3 is used in place of combs for straight line work in connection with the other two rollers; this roller is made with three sizes of combs. Anyone possessing a set of our improved graining rollers can, with a few minutes practice, do a good job of graining and imitate natural wood so that it would be almost impossible to distinguish the natural grain of any wood from the grain made by our improved wood grainers. Complete instructions packed with every set. Shipping weight, 12 ounces.
No. 30A2964 Price, per set of 3 rollers. 95c

Extra Oak Graining Roller.

Extra Graining Roller, 8 inches wide, for graining large panels.
Shipping weight, 8 ounces.
No. 30A2960 Price. 70c

The Home Wood Grainer.

A handy tool for graining wainscoting, floors, woodwork, furniture, doors, etc. You need no experience. Anyone can do graining with this grainer. All that you require is a can of the graining color, a small quantity of turpentine or benzine and one of these grainers. Width, 3 inches. Shipping wt., 7 oz.
No. 30A2965 Price. 28c

Extra Graining Roller, 3 inches wide, for graining doors, doors, woodwork, wainscoting, furniture, etc. Shipping weight, 5 ounces.
No. 30A2962 Price..... 28c

Steel Grainers.

Genuine Henry H. Taylor's English Graining Combs. The expert painter knows the quality of these combs. Sets of twelve assorted, 1 to 4 inches in tin compartment case. Shipping wt. 13 ounces.
No. 30A2966
Price, per set........... 85c

HENRY H. TAYLOR'S GRAINING COMBS FAMED FOR EXCELLENCE

Check Graining Roller.

This tool is used by the professional grainer for producing the oak overgrain on hand or rubber roller graining. Surfaces must be grained before this tool can be used. Shipping weight, 8 ounces.
No. 30A2968 Price, each................ 50c

Graining Outfit Complete, $2.55.

Your doors and woodwork can be so grained as to imitate beautiful oak. It is easy to do a good job of graining with this outfit. It is complete with material enough to cover the floor around the rugs of two large rooms, 10x10 feet. The outfit contains the following first class materials, with full directions for applying:
1 Set Special Wood Grainers, including two rollers and a Steel Graining Comb.
1 Rubberset Paint Brush, 2½ inches wide.
1 Rubberset Varnish Brush, 2 inches wide.
1 Quart Oak Ground Color.
1 Pint Golden Oak Graining Color, mixed ready for use.
1 Quart High Grade Extra Durable Floor Varnish.
These materials if bought separately would cost much more than the price we ask. Shipping weight, about 16 pounds.
No. 30A2977 Price, complete outfit. $2.55
For additional graining material order:
No. 30A2697 Ground Color.
Per quart (Shipping weight, 4 pounds)...... 58c
No. 30A2723 High Grade Extra Durable Floor Varnish.
Per quart (Shipping weight, 4 pounds)...... 63c

SEROCO PAINT — VARNISH — GROUND COLOR — COLORS IN OIL

SELECT BIBLIOGRAPHY

This bibliography is arranged by subject category so the resources are easy to find. The overall categories with their sub-categories are:

General — titles on art, architecture, interior decoration, decorative arts, historic preservation, general reference.

Decorative Painting — stencilling, infill painting, freehand painting, graining, marbling, paint, paint materials, painters, color, decorative design, ornamental decoration.

Trade Catalogs — paint, colors, stencilling, graining, decorative design.

Texas — titles and manuscripts that pertain to the history of Texas, including culture, cities, ethnic nationalities, painters and artists, architecture.

Residential Structures — sources related to individual homes.

Religious Structures — information related to the individual structures, as well as religious buildings in general.

Commercial Structures — information related to the individual structures.

City Directories and Newspapers — references that shed light on various painters and decorated structures across the state.

Interviews — owners or renters of structures, family relatives, local resource people, subject experts.

Public Records — Birth, cemetery, census, death, deed, marriage, naturalization, and will and probate records on artists, owners, and relatives listed by county.

General

Ames, Kenneth. *Beyond Necessity, Art in the Folk Tradition*. Winterthur, Delaware: The Winterthur Museum, 1977.

Arnason, H. H. *History of Modern Art*. New York: Harry N. Abrams, Inc., n. d.

Art In Our Time, New York Museum of Modern Art Catalogue, 10th Anniversary Exhibition. New York: Museum of Modern Art, 1939.

Art Nouveau, An Anthology of Design and Illustration from The Studio. New York: Dover Publications, Inc., 1969.

Arwas, Victor. *Art Deco*. New York: Harry N. Abrams, Inc., 1980.

Baigell, Matthew. *The American Scene, American Painting of the* 1930s. New York: Praeger Publishers, 1974.

Battersby, Martin. *The Decorative Thirties*. New York: Walker and Co., 1971.

Bishop, Robert and Patricia Coblentz. *The World of Antiques, Art, and Architecture in Victorian America*. New York: E. P. Dutton, 1979.

Bridgeman, Harriet, and Elizabeth Drury, editors. *The Encyclopedia of Victoriana*. New York: Macmillan Publishing Co., Inc., 1975.

Bruce, Edward and Forbes Watson. *Art in Federal Buildings*, vol. 1: *Mural Designs, 1934 – 1936*. Washington, D. C.: Art in Federal Buildings, Inc., 1936.

Bullock, Orin M. *The Restoration Manual*. Norwalk, Connecticut: Silvermine Publishers, Inc. by Atkin Productions, 1966.

Clark, Robert Judson, editor. *The Arts and Crafts*

Movement in America 1876 – 1916. Princeton, New Jersey: Princeton University Press, 1972.

Decorative Ironwork. London and New York: Paul Hamlyn, 1966.

Fales, Dean A., Robert Bishop, and Cyril I. Nelson. *American Painted Furniture 1660 – 1880*. New York: E. P. Dutton and Co., Inc., 1972.

Fitch, James Marston. *American Building: The Historical Forces that Shaped It*. New York: Schoeken Books, 2nd edition, 1977.

Fowler, John and John Cornforth. *English Decoration in the 18th Century*. London: Barrie and Jenkins, 1974.

Gowans, Alan. *Images of American Living*. Philadelphia and New York: J. B. Lippincott Co., 1964.

Gebhard, David. *Tulsa Art Deco, an Architectural Era, 1925 – 1942*. Tulsa, Oklahoma: The Junior League of Tulsa, Inc., 1980.

Greysmith, Brenda. *Wallpaper*. New York: Macmillan Publishing Co. Inc., 1976.

Guide and History, Parts 1, 2, and 3, *American Guide Series*. Dallas: Writers Program of the Works Projects Administration, Federal Works Agency, 1940.

Harding, James. *The Pre-Raphaelites*. New York: Rizzoli International Publications, Inc., 1977.

Heller, Nancy and Julia Williams. *The Regionalists*. New York: Watson-Guptill Publications, 1976.

"Historic Preservation Grants-in-Aid, for Acquisition and Development Projects." The Office of Archeology and Historic Preservation, Heritage Conservation and Recreation Service, U. S. Department of the Interior, Washington, D. C.

Hitchcock, Henry Russell. *The Pelican History of Art, Architecture: Nineteenth and Twentieth Centuries*. New York: Penguin Books, 1977, 1978.

Jensen, Robert and Patricia Conway. *Ornamentalism*. New York: Clarkson N. Potter Publications, 1982.

Johnson, Diane Chalmers. *American Art Nouveau*. New York: Harry N. Abrams, Inc., 1979.

Kidney, Walter C. *The Architecture of Choice: Eclecticism in America, 1880 – 1930*. New York: George Braziller, 1974.

Larkin, Oliver. *Art and Life in America*. New York: Holt, Rinehart, and Winston, 1946, 1960.

Latham, Ian, editor. *New Free Style, Arts and Crafts, Art Nouveau, Secession*. Great Britain: Architectural Design and Academy Editions, 1980.

"The Lindens." *Antiques*, vol. 115, no. 4. April 1979.

Lipman, Jean and Alice Winchester. *The Flowering of American Folk Art, 1776 – 1876*. New York:

The Viking Press with the Whitney Museum of American Art, 1974.

Lowe, David. *Chicago Interiors*. Chicago: Contemporary Books, Inc., 1979.

Lynes, Russell. *The Tastemakers, The Shaping of American Popular Taste*. New York: Dover Publications, Inc., 1949, 1980.

Lynn, Catherine. *Wallpaper in America*. New York: A Barra Foundation, Cooper-Hewitt Museum Book, W. W. Norton and Co., 1980.

Maas, John. *The Victorian Home in America*. New York: Hawthorn Books, Inc., 1972.

McClaugherty, Martha Crabill. "Household Art: Creating the Artistic Home, 1868 – 1893." *Winterthur Portfolio*, vol. 18, no. 1. Chicago: The University of Chicago Press, Spring 1983.

McClinton, Katherine Morrison. *Art Deco, A Guide for Collectors*. New York: Clarkson N. Potter, 1972.

McKinzie, Richard D. *The New Deal for Artists*. Princeton, New Jersey: Princeton University Press, 1973.

Moss, Roger. *Century of Color, Exterior Decoration for American Buildings, 1820 – 1920*. Watkins Glen, New York: American Life Foundation, 1981.

Naylor, Gillian. *The Arts and Crafts Movement*. Cambridge, Massachusetts: M.I.T. Press, 1971.

O'Connor, Francis V. *Art for the Millions; Essays from the 1930s by Artists and Administrators of the WPA Federal Art Project*. Greenwich, Connecticut.: New York Graphic Society, 1973.

O'Connor, Francis V., ed. *The New Deal Art Projects, An Anthology of Memoirs*. Washington, D. C.: Smithsonian Institution, 1972.

Oman, Charles O. and Jean Hamilton. *Wallpapers*. New York: Harry N. Abrams, Inc., with the Victoria and Albert Museum, London, 1982.

Pevsner, Nicholas. *The Sources of Modern Architecture and Design*. New York: Oxford University Press, 1968.

Pildas, Ave and Lucinda Smith. *Movie Palaces*. New York: Clarkson N. Potter, Inc., 1980.

Rambusch, Harold W. "The Decorations of the Theater." *American Theaters of Today*. New York: Architectural Book Publishers, 1930.

Rose, Barbara. *American Art Since 1900*. New York and Washington: Frederick A. Praeger, Publishers, 1967.

Seale, William. *Recreating the Historic House Interior*. Nashville: American Association for State and Local History, 1979.

Seale, William. *The Tasteful Interlude*. New York: Praeger Publishers, 1975.

Sexton, R. W., editor. *American Theatres of Today: Plans, Sections, and Photographs of Exterior and Interior Details.* New York: Architectural Book Publishers, 1930.

Stillinger, Elizabeth. *The Antiques Guide to Decorative Arts in America.* New York: E. P. Dutton, 1973.

Stillman, Damie. *Decorative Work of Robert Adam.* London: Academy Editions and New York: St. Martin's Press, 1973.

"The Unexpected Visitor." *Godey's Lady's Book and Magazine,* vol. 58, January 1859.

Union List of Serials in Libraries of The United States and Canada. Third Edition, vol. 4, N – R.

Van Ravenswaay, Charles. *The Arts and Architecture of German Settlements in Missouri.* Columbia: University of Missouri Press, 1977.

Verneuil, Maurice P. *Etude de la Plante,* 1906. Available at the Cooper-Hewitt Museum Library, New York, and the Architecture Library, University of Texas at Austin.

Vinci, John. *The Art Institute of Chicago: The Stock Exchange Trading Room.* Chicago: The Art Institute of Chicago, 1977.

Watkinson, Ray. *William Morris as Designer.* New York: Reinhold Publishing Corporation, 1967.

Webster, T. and Mrs. Parkes. *An Encyclopedia of Domestic Economy.* New York: Harper & Brothers, 1849.

Welsh, Peter C. *American Folk Art: The Art and Spirit of a People.* Washington, D. C.: Smithsonian Institution, 1965.

Whiffen, Marcus. *American Architecture Since 1780: A Guide to the Styles.* Cambridge, Massachusetts: M.I.T. Press, 1969, 1981.

Yarwood, Doreen. *The Architecture of Europe.* New York: Hastings House, 1974.

Yasko, Karl. "New Deal Art." Washington, D. C.: General Services Administration, n. d.

Decorative Painting

Archival Files:

New York: Cooper-Hewitt Museum, Metropolitan Museum. Paris: Forney Library. Philadelphia: Athenaeum. Wilmington, Delaware: Eleutherian Mills Historical Library.

Armstrong, Hodgson, and Delamotte. *Modern Painting, Hardwood Finishing and Sign Writing.* Chicago: Frederick J. Drake and Co. for Sears, Roebuck, and Co., 1913.

Audsley, George Ashdown. *The Practical Decorator and Ornamentalist.* Glasgow: Blackie and Son, Ltd., 189?.

Batcheler, Penelope Hartshorne. "Paint Color Research and Restoration." Technical Leaflet 15, American Association of State and Local History. *History News,* vol. 23, no. 10, October 1968.

Bearn, J. Gauld. *The Chemistry of Paints, Pigments & Varnishes.* London: n.p., n.d.

Bishop, Adele and Cile Lord. *The Art of Decorative Stencilling.* New York: Viking Press, 1976 and Penguin Books, 1978.

Bishop, Robert. *Folk Painters of America.* New York: E. P. Dutton, 1979.

Boyce, A. P. *Modern Ornamenter and Interior Decorator.* Boston: A. Williams and Co., 1874.

Callingham, James. *The Painter and Grainer's Handbook.* London: Brodie and Middleton, Simpkin, Marshall and Co., 1885.

Campana, D. M. *Decorative Designs for Decorations of All Kinds.* Chicago: D. M. Campana, 1915.

Condit, Charles L. *Painting and Painters' Materials.* New York: The Railroad Gazette, 1883.

Davidson, Ellis A. *A Practical Manual of House Painting, Graining, Marbling and Sign Writing.* London: Crosby Lockwood and Son, 1900.

"Decorative Design." *The Colorist,* vol. 4, no. 6. Cleveland: Sherwin-Williams Paint Co., July-August, 1911.

Downs, Arthur Channing, Jr. "Zinc for Paint and Architectural Use in the 19th Century." *Bulletin of The Association for Preservation Technology,* vol. 8, no. 4. Ottawa, Ontario: 1976.

Dresser, Christopher. *The Art of Decorative Design.* London: Day and Son, 1862; reprinted Watkins Glen, New York: American Life Foundation, 1977.

Dresser, Christopher. *Development of Ornamental Art in the International Exhibition.* London: Day and Son, 1862.

Dresser, Christopher. *Principles of Decorative Design.* New York: St. Martin's Press and London: Academy Editions, 1973 (reprint of 1873 London edition by Cassell, Petter and Galpin).

Dresser, Christopher. *Studies in Design.* London: Cassell, Petter and Galpin, 1876.

Exterior Decoration. New York: F. W. Devoe and Co. and Chicago: Coffin, Devoe, and Co., 1885.

Gardner, F. B. *Everybody's Paint Book.* New York: M. T. Richardson, Publisher, 1884, 1886.

Gardner, F. B. *How to Paint.* New York: Samuel R. Wells, publisher, 1872; reprinted Watkins Glen, New York: The American Life Foundation, Library of Victorian Culture, 1978.

Gardner, Franklin B. *The Painters' Encyclopedia.* New York: M. T. Richardson Co., Publishers, 1906.

Grinnell, V. B. *Grinnell's Handbook on Painting.* Vinton, Iowa: n.p., 1894.

Haney's Manual of Sign, Carriage and Decorative Painting. New York: Excelsior Publishing House, 1870.

Harwood, Buie. "Fancy the Ornament: Decorative Painting in Texas, 1840s–1940s." *Texas Architect,* vol. 30, no. 5, September-October 1980.

Harwood, Buie, and Betty McKee. "Reproduction of Historic Decorative Ceilings and Wall Friezes in Texas." *Journal of Interior Design Education and Research,* vol. 4, no. 1, Spring 1978. Later published by permission in *Perspective* (publication of the Society of Architectural Historians-Texas Chapter), vol. 7, no. 3–4, December 1979.

Harwood, Buie. "Stencilling: Interior Architectural Ornamentation." *Journal of Interior Design Education and Research,* vol. 12, no. 1, Fall 1986.

Henderson, Lana, "Decorative Painting: An Endangered Treasure." *Texas Homes,* December 1982.

Hasluck, Paul N., editor. *House Decoration.* London, Paris, New York, Toronto, Melbourne: Cassell and Co., Ltd., 1894–1908.

Higgins, W. Mullingar. *The House Painter or, Decorator's Companion: Being a Complete Treatise on the Origin of Colour, the Laws of Harmonious Colouring, the Manufacture of Pigments, Oils, and Varnishes; and the Art of House Painting, Graining, and Marbling. To Which is Added, A History of the Art in All Ages.* London: Thomas Kelly, Paternoster Row, 1861.

Home Painting Manual. Cleveland: Sherwin-Williams and Co., 1922.

House Painting and Decorating. A Journal Devoted to the House Painter and the Decorator, vol. 2, October 1886 – September 1887. Philadelphia: The House Painting and Decorating Publishing Co., 1887.

"The House We Live In." New York: The National Lead Company, 1920.

Jennings, Arthur Seymour. *The Modern Painter and Decorator, a practical work on house painting and decorating,* vol. 2. London: The Caxton Publishing Co., Ltd., n. d. (ca. 1900).

Jones, Owen. *The Grammar of Ornament.* New York: Van Nostrand Reinhold Co., 1982 (reprint of 1856 British edition).

Kelly, A. Ashmun. *The Standard Grainer, Stainer and Marbler.* Philadelphia: David McKay, 1923.

Kelly, Kenneth L. and Deane B. Judd. *Color, Universal Language and Dictionary of Names.* National Bureau of Standards Special Publication 440. Washington, D. C.: U. S. Department of Commerce, Government Printing Office, December 1976.

Little, Nina Fletcher. *Itinerant Painting in America, 1750–1850.* Cooperstown, New York: Farmers' Museum, 1949.

Lowndes, William. *Painting and Wood Finishing.* n.p.: n. p., 1926.

Maire, F. *Modern Painters' Cyclopedia.* Chicago: Frederick J. Drake and Co. Publishers, 1910, 1918.

Marling, Karal Ann. *Wall-to-Wall America.* Minneapolis: University of Minnesota Press, 1982.

Masury, John W. *The American Grainers' Handbook: A Popular and Practical Treatise on the Art of Imitating Colored and Fancy Woods; With Examples and Illustrations, Both in Oil and Distemper.* New York: John W. Masury and Son, 1872.

Masury, John W. *House-Painting, Carriage-Painting, and Graining.* New York: D. Appleton and Co., 1881.

Masury, John W. A *Popular Treatise on the Art of House Painting: Plain and Decorative.* New York: D. Appleton and Co., 1868.

Meyer, Franz Sales. A *Handbook of Ornament.* London: Duckworth and Co., 1974 (from a book first published in Leipzig in 1888; first appeared in America in 1892).

Miller, Fred. *Interior Decoration: A Practical Treatise on Surface Decoration, with Notes on Colour, Stencilling, and Panel Painting.* London: E. Menken, ca. 1885.

Minhinnick, Jeanne. "Some Personal Observations on the Use of Paint in Early Ontario." *Bulletin of The Association for Preservation Technology,* vol. 7, no. 2, 1975.

Mitchell, F. Scott. A *Few Suggestions for Ornamental Decoration: A Collection of Designs and Colour Schemes for Painter's and Decorator's Work.* London: Thomas Parsons and Sons, 1908.

Osborne, Louis Allen. *Painting and Interior Decoration.* Philadelphia: David McKay Co., 1925.

The Painter: An Illustrated Monthly Magazine Devoted to Painting and Decoration, vol. 4. Cleveland: The Painting Co., January-December 1885.

The Painter, Gilder, and Varnisher's Companion. Philadelphia: Henry Carey Baird, 1871.

"The Painter of the Nineteenth Century — An Appreciation." *The Colorist.* Cleveland: Sherwin-Williams Paint Co., 1912.

The Painters Magazine (and Coach Painter or Wallpaper Trade Journal), New York, vol. 13, no. 10, October 1886; vol. 14, no. 6, June 1887; vol. 15, no. 3, March 1888; vol. 15, no. 4, April 1888; vol.

16, no. 8, August 1889; vol. 17, no. 10, October 1890; vol. 18, no. 3, March 1891; vol. 32, no. 6, June 1905.

"Painting as a Career." *The Colorist*, vol. 4, no. 4. Cleveland: Sherwin-Williams Paint Co., May, 1911.

Phillips, Morgan and Norman R. Weiss. "Some Notes on Paint Research and Reproduction." *Bulletin of The Association for Preservation Technology*, vol. 7, no. 4., 1975.

Phillips, Morgan W. "Discoloration of Old House Paints: Restoration of Paint Colors at the Harrison Gray Otis House, Boston." *Paint Color Research and Restoration of Historic Paint*. Reprinted from *The Bulletin of The Association for Preservation Technology*. Publication Supplement, September 1977.

The Popular Art Instructor. Windsor and Toronto, Ontario: J. B. Young and Co. Publishers, 1887.

"Practical Application of Design." *The Colorist*, vol. 4, no. 6. Cleveland: Sherwin-Williams Paint Co., July-August, 1911.

Pugin, Augustus Welby. *Floriated Ornament*. London: Henry G. Bohn, 1849.

Rapp, Conrad. *Marbleizing: The New Method*. New York: by the author, 1952.

Ritz, Josef M. and Gisland M. Ritz. *Alte Bemalte Bauermobel*. Munchen: Verlag Georg D. W. Callwey, 1975.

Romaine, Lawrence B. *A Guide to American Trade Catalogs, 1744 – 1900*. New York: n.p., 1960.

Standard Method of Specifying Color by the Munsell System, #D-1535 – 80. Philadelphia: American Society for Testing Materials, December 1980.

Strange, E. F. "Stencilling as an Art." *The Studio, An Illustrated Magazine of Fine and Applied Art*, vol. 3. London: Ballantyne, Hanson and Co., April, 1894.

The Studio, An Illustrated Magazine of Fine and Applied Art, vol. 12; vol. 19. London: Ballantyne, Hanson and Co., October 1897, February 1900.

Tingry, P. F. *The Painter's and Colourman's Complete Guide: Being a Practical and Theoretical Treatise on the Preparation of Colours, and Their Application to the Different Kinds of Painting: in Which is Particularly Described the Whole Art of House Painting*. London: Sherwood, Gilbert and Piper, 1830.

Toch, Maximilan. *Materials for Permanent Painting: A Manual for Manufacturers, Art Dealers, Artists, and Collectors*. New York: D. Van Nostrand Co., 1911.

Towndes, William S. *Painting and Wood Finishing*.

Scranton, Pennsylvania: International Textbook Co., 1926.

Treasury of Art Nouveau Design and Ornament. Selected by Carol Belanger Grafton. New York: Dover Publications, Inc., 1980.

Vanderwalker, F. N. *Interior Wall Decoration: Practical Working Methods for Plain and Decorative Finishes, New and Standard Treatments*. Chicago: Frederick J. Drake and Co., Publishers, 1924.

Vanderwalker, F. N. *New Stencils and Their Use*. Chicago: Frederick J. Drake and Co., Publishers, 1918.

Vanderwalker, F. N., editor. *Painting and Decorating, Working Methods*. The International Association of Master House Painters and Decorators of the United States and Canada, 1922, 2nd edition.

Volz, John. "Paint Bibliography." *Paint Color Research and Restoration of Historic Paint*, Publication Supplement. Ottawa, Ontario: The Association for Preservation Technology, September 1977.

Wall, William E. *Graining, Ancient and Modern*. Chicago: Frederick J. Drake and Co., 1937.

Wall, William E. *Practical Graining*. Philadelphia: House Painting and Decorating Publishing Co., 1891.

Waring, Janet. *Early American Stencils on Walls and Furniture*. New York: Dover Publications, 1968.

Warren, W. C. *The House and Sign Painters' Recipe Book*. Noblesville, Indiana: n.p., 1890.

Welsh, Frank. "Report on Early Wall Stencil in Philadelphia." *Bulletin of The Association for Preservation Technology*, vol. 5, no. 2, 1973.

The Western Painter, selected volumes. Chicago: 1892.

Whittock, Nathaniel. *The Decorative Painters' and Glaziers' Guide*. London: Isaac Taylor Hinton, 1827.

Winkler, Gail Casey, and Roger W. Moss. *Victorian Interior Decoration: American Interiors, 1830 – 1900*. New York: Henry Holt and Co., 1986.

Trade Catalogs

Alabastine Paint Company, Grand Rapids, Michigan, ca. early 20th century. Water Base Paints, "Better than Kalsomine"; 12 colors.

Birge, M. H. and Sons, Buffalo, New York, ca. 1885. "Calesco"; "Oil Bound — Water Paint — Washable"; 40 colors. ca. 1922.

Callow, J. J. "Graining Tools." Cleveland, Ohio: ca. 1900

Diamond Wall Finish Company, Water Base Paints, Gypsine, "A Superior Substitute for Kalsomine"; 10 colors. Grand Rapids, Michigan: ca. 1890.

"Excelsior Fresco Stencils." Chicago: Chicago Stencil Co., ca. 1900. Also listed with the name of a Mr. H. Roessing.

"Free Alabastine Stencils." Grand Rapids, Michigan: Alabastine Co., ca. 1900.

"Illustrated Catalogue and Price List, Stencil Treasury." New York: A. Wiggers, 215 E. 59th St., ca. 1895.

H. W. Johns Manufacturing Company. Boston: ca. February 1894.

"Sereco Paint Catalog." Chicago: Sears, Roebuck and Co., 1911, 1915, 1918.

"Stencils and Stencil Material." Cleveland: Sherwin-Williams Co., 1910, 1918.

"Suggestions in Decorative Design." London: William Harland, ca. 1894.

Texas

Agatha, Sister M. *History of the Heights 1891 – 1918.* n.p.: Premier Printing Co., 1956.

Alexander, Drury Blakely. *Texas Homes of the 19th Century.* Austin: University of Texas Press for the Amon Carter Museum of Western Art, 1966

Art Work of Galveston. Chicago: W. H. Parish Publishing Co., 1894.

Barnstone, Howard. *The Galveston That Was.* New York: MacMillan Co., and Houston: The Museum of Fine Arts, 1966.

Biesle, Rudolph Leopold. *History of German Settlements in Texas, 1831 – 1861.* Austin: Van Boeckman-Jones Co., 1930.

Chabot, Frederick C. *Genealogies of Early San Antonio Families (The Makers of San Antonio).* San Antonio: Artes Graficas, 1937.

Dietrich, Wilfred C. *The Blazing Story of Washington County.* Brenham: n.p., 1950.

Early-Day History of Wilbarger County. Vernon: *The Vernon Daily Record,* 1933 – 1973; copyright, The Wilbarger Historical Survey Committee.

Easley, S. C. *Early Texas Birth Records: 1833 – 1878.* n.p.: Southern Historical Press, 1978.

Engelbrecht, Lloyd C. and June-Marie Engelbrecht. *Henry C. Trost: Architect of the Southwest.* El Paso: El Paso Public Library Association, 1981.

Everett, Donald E. *San Antonio: The Flavor of Its Past, 1845 – 1898.* San Antonio: Trinity Press, 1975.

Flury, Dorothy Agnes. *Our Father, Godfrey: A Biography.* Austin: Hart Graphics and Office Centers, Inc., 1976.

Forrester-O'Brien, Esse. *Art and Artists in Texas.* Dallas: Tardy Publishing Co., 1935.

Gideon, Samuel E. *Historic and Picturesque Austin.* Austin: The Steck Co., 1936.

Goeldner, Paul. *Texas Catalog, Historic American Buildings Survey.* Edited by Lucy Pope Wheeler and S. Allen Chambers, Jr. San Antonio: Trinity University Press, 1974.

Greater San Antonio: The City of Destiny and of Your Destination. San Antonio: Higher Publicity League of Texas, 1918.

Harwood, Buie. "A Force for the Future: Preservation Education, Case Study — Interior Design, Winedale Institute in Historic Preservation, The University of Texas at Austin." *Journal of Interior Design Education and Research,* vols. 5 – 6, nos. 1 – 2, Fall 1979, Spring 1980.

Hasskarl, Robert A., Jr. *Brenham, Texas, 1844 – 1958.* Brenham: Brenham Banner Press Publishing Co., 1958.

"History of the Heights" (Scrapbook). vol. 1, Summer 1955. Houston Public Library, Texas Collection.

Horgan, Paul. *Peter Hurd: A Portrait Sketch From Life.* Fort Worth: Amon Carter Museum of Western Art and Austin: University of Texas Press, 1965.

"Houston Buildings. " Houston Public Library, Texas Collection (City Hall clippings file).

"Houston Buildings and Architecture." Houston Public Library, Texas Collection (Scrapbooks, vols. A – Z, clippings from newspapers and other sources, mounted prior to January 1963).

Jordan, Terry G. *German Seed in Texas Soil: Immigrant Farmers in Nineteenth Century Texas.* Austin: University of Texas Press, 1966.

Key, Della Tyler. *In the Cattle Country: History of Potter County, 1887 – 1966.* Quanah and Wichita Falls: Nortex Offset Publications, Inc., 1972.

The Last of the Past, Houston Architecture, 1847 – 1915: An Inventory and Architectural Stylistic History of remaining early commercial buildings. Houston: n.p., 1980.

Lich, Glen E. *The German Texans.* San Antonio: University of Texas Institute of Texan Cultures, 1981.

McDonald, William L. *Dallas Rediscovered: A Photographic Chronicle of Urban Expansion 1870 – 1925.* Dallas: Dallas Historical Society, 1978.

Partlow, Miriam. *Liberty, Liberty County and the Atascosito District.* Austin: The Pemberton Press, Jenkins Publishing Co., 1974.

Pannington, Mrs. R. E. *History of Brenham and Washington County, Texas.* Houston: Standard Printing and Lithographing Co., 1915.

Robinson, Willard B. *Texas Public Buildings of the Nineteenth Century.* Austin: University of Texas Press for the Amon Carter Museum of Western Art, 1974.

The Standard Blue Book of Texas: Who's Who, 1907 – 1908. Houston: Who's Who Publishing Co., 1907.

Taylor, Lonn. *Texas Furniture.* Austin: University of Texas Press, 1975.

Texas, A Guide to the Lone Star State. American Guide Series. New York: Hasting House Publishers, 1940.

"Texas Art and Artists." (Scrapbooks, vols. A – Z) Houston Public Library, Texas Collection.

The Texians and The Texans. Series of pamphlets on Texas history including "The Afro-American Texans," "The Italian Texans," "The Anglo-American Texans," "The French Texans," "The Norwegian Texans," "The Polish Texans," "The Spanish Texans," and "The Czech Texans." San Antonio: University of Texas Institute of Texan Cultures, 1973 – 1981.

Tom Lea: A Selection of Paintings and Drawings from the Nineteen-Sixties. San Antonio: Institute of Texan Cultures, University of Texas, 1969.

Williamson, Roxanne Ruter. *Austin, Texas: An American Architectural History.* San Antonio: Trinity University Press, 1973.

Winfield, Nat, Jr., and Judy Winfield. *Cemetery Records of Washington County, 1826 – 1960.* Brenham: n.p., 1974.

Withers, Daniel. *San Antonio: A History of Color and Graphics.* San Antonio: San Antonio Conservation Society, 1977.

Zwiener, Douglas R. and Elisabeth Darst. *A Guide to Historic Galveston.* Galveston: n.p., 1966.

Residential Structures

Allen, James. "Voices from the Past." Unpublished research paper on the Bivins House, August 1972 (Amarillo Public Library).

Archival Files:

Austin: Barker Texas History Center, Franklin Savings Association, Hoffman Architects, Texas Historical Commission (National Register of Historic Places). Brenham: Sander Family History. Dallas: Meadows Foundation. Fort Worth: Wharton-Scott House. Houston: Meister Family Papers, Sam Houston Historical Park. Johnson City: National Park Service. Round Top: Winedale Historical Center. San Antonio: Landa Library, San Antonio Conservation Society. Wichita Falls: Wichita County Historical Society.

Alter, Judy. *Thistle Hill: The History and the House.* Fort Worth: Texas Christian University Press, 1988.

Brooks, Sarah E. "Charles Martin Meister, 1875 – 1935." Unpublished research paper, 1980 (author's collection).

Harwood, Buie. "Charles Martin Meister: Decorative Painter in Texas." *Journal of Interior Design Education and Research,* vol. 7, no. 2, 1981.

Landa, Harry. *As I Remember.* San Antonio: Carleton Printing Co., 1945.

Porter, Rose McCoy. *Thistle Hill: The Cattle Baron's Legacy.* Fort Worth: Branch-Smith, Inc., 1980.

Ramsey, Buck. "Lee Bivins — Cattleman." *Accent West.* November 1979 – January 1980.

Shuffler, Henderson. "Winedale Inn, An Early Texas Cultural Crossroad." *The Texas Quarterly.* vol. 8, no. 2., 1965.

Suttle, Catherine. "Texas Craftsman: A Study of the L. T. Wright House, San Antonio, Texas." Unpublished research paper, May 1980 (author's collection).

Taylor, Lonn. "The McGregor-Grimm House at Winedale, Texas." reprinted from *Antiques.* New York: September 1975.

Religious Structures

Archival Files:

Amarillo: First Baptist Church. Austin: Catholic Archives of Texas, Hoffman Architects, Texas Historical Commission (National Register of Historic Places), University of Texas (Architectural Drawings Collection). Canyon: Panhandle Plains Museum (Guy Carlander Collection). Fredricksburg: St. Mary's Catholic Church. Galveston-Houston: Catholic Archives, Rosenberg Library. Lindsay: St. Peter's Catholic Church. Montreat, North Carolina: Presbytere Archives. Moravia: Ascension Catholic Church. San Antonio: Catholic Archives, Library of the Daughters of the Republic of Texas at the Alamo (Diehlmann and Schuchard Collections), Our Lady of the Lake University. Wallis: Guardian Angel Church.

Barnes, Lavonia Jenkins. *19th Century Churches in Texas.* Waco: Texian Press, 1982.

Blasig, Anne. *The Wends of Texas.* San Antonio: The Naylor Co., 1954.

Butler, Linda Flory, with Carol Kennedy and Buie Harwood (consultant). "Churches in Texas with Decorative Painting." National Register of Historic Places Thematic Nomination. Austin: Texas Historical Commission, 1983.

Castaneda, Carlos E. *Our Catholic Heritage in*

Texas, 1519 – 1936, vols. 6 and 7. New York: Arno Press, 1976.

Driskill, Frank A. and Noel Grisham. *Historic Churches of Texas.* Burnet, Texas: Eakin Press, 1980.

Flory, Linda C. "Historical Study of Wesley Brethren Church, Wesley, Texas." Unpublished research paper, 1978 (author's collection).

Freeman-Doty Associates. *Wesley Brethren Church, Historic Structures Report.* Wesley: Privately published, 1980.

Gittinger, Ted and Connie Rihn, Roberta Haby, Charlene Snavely. *St. Louis Church, Castroville.* San Antonio: Graphic Arts, 1973.

Grider, Sylvia A. *The Wendish Texans.* San Antonio: University of Texas Institute of Texas Cultures, 1982.

Harwood, Buie. "Painted Church Decoration in Texas: Articulating an Art and a Style." *Perspective* (publication of the Society of Architectural Historians-Texas Chapter), vol. 12, no. 2, Fall 1983.

Harwood, Buie. "Painted Church Decoration in Texas, Part II: A Closer View of Ornamentation." *Perspective,* vol. 13, no. 2, Spring 1985.

Mason, Herbert Malloy, Jr. "Missions of Texas." *Southern Living.* Birmingham, Alabama: Oxmoor House, Inc. 1974 (undated, copy at Catholic Archives of Texas, Austin).

McDermott, Rev. D. I. "The Use of Holy Pictures and Images." *Cabinet of Catholic Information.* New York: Murphy and McCarthy, 1903.

Neuman, Ray. *A Centennial History of St. Joseph's Church and Parish, 1868 to 1968, San Antonio, Texas.* San Antonio: Clemons Printing Co., 1968.

Noonan-Guerra, Mary Ann. *San Fernando, Heart of San Antonio.* San Antonio: Francis J. Fury, 1977.

Parvin, Bob. "Old San Fernando." *Texas Highways.* November 1977.

Pierce, Richard. "Maticka Praha." *Texas Highways.* December 1974.

Repp, Arthur G. "St. Paul's and St. Peter's Lutheran Churches, Serbin, Texas, 1855 – 1905." *Concordia Historical Institute Quarterly,* vols. 15, 16, 17 (Barker Texas History Center, University of Texas at Austin).

Thomas, Les. "Painted Churches Shine with Tradition." *Southern Living,* December 1984.

Webber, F. R. *Church Symbolism.* Cleveland: J. H. Jansen, 1927, 1938.

Whittemore, Caroll E., editor. *Symbols of the Church.* Boston: Whittemore Associates, n.d.

Commercial Structures

Archival Files:

Alvin: Alvin Museum Society. Austin: Austin Public Library (Austin-Travis County Collection), Barker Texas History Center (Battle Papers and University of Texas Architectural Drawings Collection). Dallas: Dallas Historical Society (Fair Park Collection, Dallas Independent School District Collection, and Robert Johnson Files), Dallas Public Library (Interstate Theaters-Martin Woods Collection, Jerry Bywaters Collection). Fort Worth: YWCA. Gatesville: Postmaster Collection. Harlingen: Normah Knight Collection. Houston: Houston Public Library (Texas Collection, Gulf Building file and Prudential Life Insurance Company Collection). Mercedes: Hidalgo County Bank and Trust. San Antonio: University of Texas Institute of Texan Cultures (Old Downtown Station Postmaster Collection, Thomas Jefferson High School file).

Blodgett, Bill. "Highland Park Village, A Bit of Barcelona." *Texas Architect,* vol. 30, no. 6, November-December 1980.

Houston Architectural Survey. *National Register Entries: User's Guide,* vol. 6, supplement. Austin: Texas Historical Commission (National Register of Historic Places), 1981.

McMichael, Carol. *Paul Cret at Texas.* Austin: Archer Huntington Art Gallery, College of Fine Arts, University of Texas, 1983.

Williamson, Roxanne. *A History of the Campus and Buildings of the University of Texas.* Austin: University of Texas. n. d.

City Directories

Amarillo City Directory, 1907.

Austin City Directory, 1932 – 1933.

Austin Telephone Directory, 1932 – 1935.

Chicago City Directory, 1874 – 1875, 1886, 1887, 1899 – 1902.

Dallas City Directory, 1929, 1932, 1933 – 1934, 1936 – 1955.

Dallas Telephone Directory, 1930, 1934 – 1947, 1956, 1964.

Galveston City Directory, 1866 – 1867, 1886 – 1887, 1889 – 1890, 1891 – 1892, 1899 – 1900.

Houston City Directory, 1889 – 1890, 1908 – 1909, 1931 – 1935.

Lakeside Business Directory of Chicago, 1893 – 1898.

San Antonio City Directory, 1891 – 1922, 1929 – 1935.

Interviews

Arndt, Mr. and Mrs. Leslie, December 1, 1982, Cuero.

Bagat, Mrs. Robert, December 10, 1982, Dickinson.

Bivins, Mrs. Lee, February 1984, Amarillo.

Boehm, Mrs. Eddie, March 17, 1982 and September 21, 1982, Lindenau.

Burrage, Col. Richard, December 6, 1982, Houston.

Burton, Mrs. Grover, June 19, 1982, McKinney.

Cariker, Joe W., superintendent at Varner-Hogg State Historical Park, March 18, 1982, West Columbia.

Chudleigh, Deborah, December 1, 1982, Weimar.

Clemons, Mr. and Mrs. Ray, October 31, 1982, Gonzales.

Cox, Roy C., December 6, 1982, Houston.

Davis, Rev. James M., November 4, 1982, Palestine.

Detering, Mrs. Carl, December 5, 1982, Hempstead.

Donecker, Mrs. Frederick W., October 1, 1983, San Antonio.

Dougherty, Mr. and Mrs. Ken, June 1979, Brenham.

Elder, Granville, Jr., December 6, 1982, Houston.

Feldhousen, Elmer, General Services Administration. February 7, 1980, Houston.

Flury, Dorothy Agnes, February 7, 1980, Austin.

Ganchen, Dick, Summer 1982, Spring and Summer 1983, Chapell Hill.

Gandy, W. H., December 6, 1982, Montgomery.

Gilboe, Rolf J., November 29, 1983, Dallas.

Grady, W. D., December 6, 1982, Houston.

Grice, Mrs. James, July 21, 1983, Navasota.

Grimm, Laura, July 3, 1981, Brenham.

Hadley, Mrs. William Florine, October 27, 1982, San Antonio.

Hagan, Hattie Meister, June 28, 1981, Houston.

Halla, Carol, July 22, 1983, Weimar.

Henzelka, Henry and Matilda, September 23, 1982, Cistern.

Herlin, Mrs. Bob, March 18, 1982, Palacios.

Hollen, Cheta, November 30, 1982, Fort Davis.

Hood, Bonnie, June 1981, Cat Spring.

Huebner, Mrs. Milton, July 22, 1983, Industry and Welcome Community.

Johnson, Mrs. Richard, July 15, 1983, Ehlinger.

Joskusch, Julius W., December 9, 1982, Galveston.

Kahlich, Edwin and Erna Olle, November 29, 1982, Lindenau.

Kahlich, Willa Marie, December 1, 1982, Lindenau.

Kaloudis, Father John, February 8, 1983, San Antonio.

Kasner, Sister Delores, September 28, 1983, at the Catholic Archives of Texas in Austin.

Kollatschny, A. G., May 16, 1984, Cat Spring.

Kruse, Mr. and Mrs. Howard, June 1979, Spring 1980, and June 1980, Brenham.

Lamon, Margaret, November 22, 1978, Lacoste.

Luerssen, Alfred B., February 9, 1983, Victoria.

Mahalia, Mrs. John, September 30, 1982, San Antonio.

Marshall, Mrs. Esther, November 18, 1978, Beckville.

McGuire, James Patrick, October 1982, San Antonio.

McManus, Father Michael, November 22, 1978, Lacoste.

Melchior, Mrs. Arthur (Elsa), May 8, 1984, Austin.

Merritt, Mr. and Mrs. Cal, June 16, 1982, McKinney.

Miller, Tom, November 5, 1982, Center.

Mikkelson, Barbara Berry, June 26, 1982, Vernon.

Montag, Mrs. Victor, correspondence dated Fall 1979, Henderson.

Parker, Herbert C., November 5, 1982, Center.

Peavler, Georgia, General Services Administration, March 1983, Fort Worth.

Perkin, Mrs. Rural, November 10, 1979, Hopewell Community near Mt. Vernon.

Poehlmann, Jeanette and Ralph, June 24 and 26, 1981, Brenham.

Psencik, Felix, and Leo Psencik, September 25, 1982, Cistern.

Quebe, Mrs. Theodore, June 27, 1981, Brenham.

Reischling, Mrs. Howard, September 23, 1982, San Antonio.

Richardson, Nan Lou, November 10, 1979, Henderson.

Roberts, Mrs. Summerfield Griffith, March 1980, Dallas.

Roehl, Mrs. Otto C. and Mr. and Mrs. Walter O. Roehl, March 17, 1982, Yorktown.

Rudy, Beverly, February 1984, Galveston.

Schuh, Jo, November 22, 1978, Lacoste.

Schwettmann, Clara Bockhorn, June 27, 1981, Brenham.

Singleton, Kate, October 1982, Dallas.

Stockert, Herman, February 9, 1983, San Antonio.

Tegeler, Mrs. Raymond, July 3, 1979, Brenham.

Van Riper, Paul P., March 14, 1982, Bryan.

Wagner, Mrs. W. J., First Baptist Church, August 13, 1982, Amarillo.

Walker, Ann, October 28, 1982, San Antonio.

Wiggin, Verdel, November 19, 1982, Harlingen.

Wilson, Mrs. Patricia S., July 15, 1983, La Grange.

Winklemann, Mrs. Albert, June 24 and 27, 1981, Brenham.

Wood, Dinky, October 1982, in Colorado.

Young, Owen, December 6, 1982 and January 26, 1983, Houston.

Zimmerhanzel, Edwin and Donna, March 15, 1982 and September 23, 1982.

Newspapers

Amarillo Daily News, October 28, 1947 ("Esquire Theater Bows in Tonight"); January 1, 1952 ("Last Rites Set for Mrs. Bivins").

Amarillo News-Globe, January 8, 1939.

Amarillo Sunday News-Globe, August 3, 1930; October 26, 1947 ("Special Stage Program to Mark Gala Opening of Family Theater").

Austin American, October 12, 1915 ("Opening of the Majestic Theater"); July 15, 1930.

Austin American Statesman, January 25, 1976 ("Walter Tips built his historic home in 1876").

Baptist Standard Newspaper, January 1, 1925; October 30, 1930; May 16, 1935.

Brenham Daily Banner, Selected Volumes 1890 – 1907.

Corpus Christi Caller-Times, September 21, 1974 ("Post Office murals saved, headed for new courthouse"); February 8, 1980 ("Rescued from post office: Old murals to be hung in Courthouse").

Dallas Morning News, May 16, 1947; October 6, 1948 ("Theatrical Landmark gets face lifted for new look"); July 28, 1949 ("New Forest Features Modern Architectural Innovations"); October 29, 1982 ("A revival of elegance and style").

Dallas News, August 22, 1937 ("Artists now teach to fill cupboards"); June 12, 1938 ("Home Region as a Source of All Art").

Dallas Times Herald, August 16, 1936 ("Two Heroic Murals in Texas Hall by American Painter").

Ft. Worth Star-Telegram and Sunday Record, May 6, 1928 ("Public Invited to Elks Club Opening"); May 7, 1928 ("New Home of Fort Worth Elks Opens for 3-Day Inspection").

The Galveston Daily News, February 26, 1889 ("New Church Dedicated"); March 18, 1970 ("Dedication of Historic Church Open to the Public Thursday").

Gatesville Messenger, February 26, 1976 ("Post Office Muralist was Never in Texas").

Hallettsville Herald, July 6, 1899.

Houston Chronicle, July 28, 1935 ("Murals in Esperson Building Lobby are ready for unveiling"); November 5, 1939; December 1, 1940 ("Elisabet Ney's Beloved Liendo opens as a Shrine to her Memory").

Houston Daily Post, February 12, 1893.

Houston Post, April 30, 1961 ("Old Stone Church Wend's Monument").

Houston Press, February 10, 1938.

Pampa Daily News, August 7, 1934.

Robstown Record, May 29, 1941 ("Post-office Mural Hung Monday Tells Matter-of-Fact Story of Cotton Empire Building"); June 5, 1941.

San Antonio Express, November 20, 1938 ("1,000 Years of Life Murals to go in Federal Building"); July 21, 1946 ("Children Ready for New Park").

San Antonio Light, July 19, 1946; July 26, 1946; February 9, 1947; December 12, 1951.

Southern Messenger, June 22, 1893 ("Dedication of the Sacred Heart Church at Palestine, Texas"); November 28, 1895 ("Blessing of the New Church and Confirmation at Praha"); April 11, 1895 ("Forty Hours' Devotion in the New Church at Westphalia"); December 15, 1904. ; September 6, 1906 ("New Church Dedicated at Fredericksburg"); October 11, 1917 ("Church at Ammansville Destroyed by Fire"); March 6, 1919 ("Father Netardus Jubilee"); June 5, 1919. ; June 12, 1919 ("New Church Dedicated at Sweet Home, Texas"); September 11, 1919 ("Shiner's New Church"); October 16, 1919 ("Church Dedicated at Lindsay, Texas"); November 13, 1919. ; December 25, 1919.

Upper Valley Progress (Mission), May 3, 1978 ("Post Office mural discovers fame").

Valley Morning Star (Harlingen), May 30, 1948 ("Mural Tells History of Bread Making"); March 25, 1951 ("Modernistic New Building Both Beautiful and Functional" and "Colorful, Exciting Mural Dominates New Bank Lobby").

Public Records

Austin County Courthouse:
Deed Records: vol. 114, no. 269, p. 391; vol 27, no. 28, p. 28: vol. 2, no. 624; vol. G, no. 436, p. 512 – 513.

Marriage Records: vol. F, no. 864, p. 437; vol. F, no. 930, p. 471.

Probate and Succession Records: vol. 14, no. 3982, File #146, pp. 441 – 446.

Austin Department of Health,
Bureau of Vital Statistics:
Death Records: Allidi #41058; Jessen #99992.

Bexar County Courthouse:
Birth Records: vol. 286, #017721, p. 608; vol. 286, #017720, p. 607; on Alfons Joseph Stockert.

Marriage Records: Book 4, #34466, p. 134; Book 78, #36209, p. 678.

Probate Records: Will #153004, Will #16212 (1928), Will #20505 (1932), Will #137084 (1973), Will #120249 (1966), Will #134390 (1972), Will #84077.
Texas Cemetery Records, Miscellaneous Bible Records. Compiled by Mr. Raymond R. Russell, Chairman, Genealogical Records Committee, Alamo Chapter, DAR. San Antonio, 1958.

Dallas City Hall:
Death Records: E. J. Gilboe #199.

Dewitt County Courthouse:
Birth Records: vol. 4, pp. 23 and 60; vol. 3, p. 95.
Probate Records: vol. 27, Will #2663, pp. 58 – 59.

Fayette County Courthouse:
Marriage Records: Book 6, December 1890 – January 1893, # 495, p. 243; Book 9, March 1899 – January 1902, #3145, p. 385; Book 10, January 1902 – November 1904, #3513, p. 89.
Probate Records: Book 2, 1880 – 1907, #1466, Book F, pp. 416, 458, 529.

Harris County Courthouse:
Probate Records: Malinde Meister, 1934 – 1935, #21973/655-50-1522; 1962 – 1969, #613-35-0400 and #615-63-0404; no will on file for Charles M. Meister.

Harris County:
Index to Naturalization Records: 1855 – 1906, #1009262; Houston Public Library, Texas Collection.
Record of Internments of the City of Galveston, 1859 – 1872. Copied by Peggy H. Gregory. Houston, 1976.

Travis County Courthouse:
Probate Records: Jessen #42. 012.

Washington County Courthouse:
Birth Records: Hattie Anna Bertha Meister, 1906.
Deed Records: Book 92, pp. 139 – 140; Book 354, #1924, pp. 409 – 411.
Marriage Records: vol. 2, p. 176; vol. 6, #252, p. 126; vol. 8, #1889, p. 461; vol. 15, #10247, p. 187.
Probate Records: Book I, McGregor, pp. 490 – 507; vol. Y, Sander will, p. 334.

Washington County:
Texas Census Schedule 1900. Precinct #3, Brenham, June 9, 1900, Sheet #9.